OLD SILVERDALE

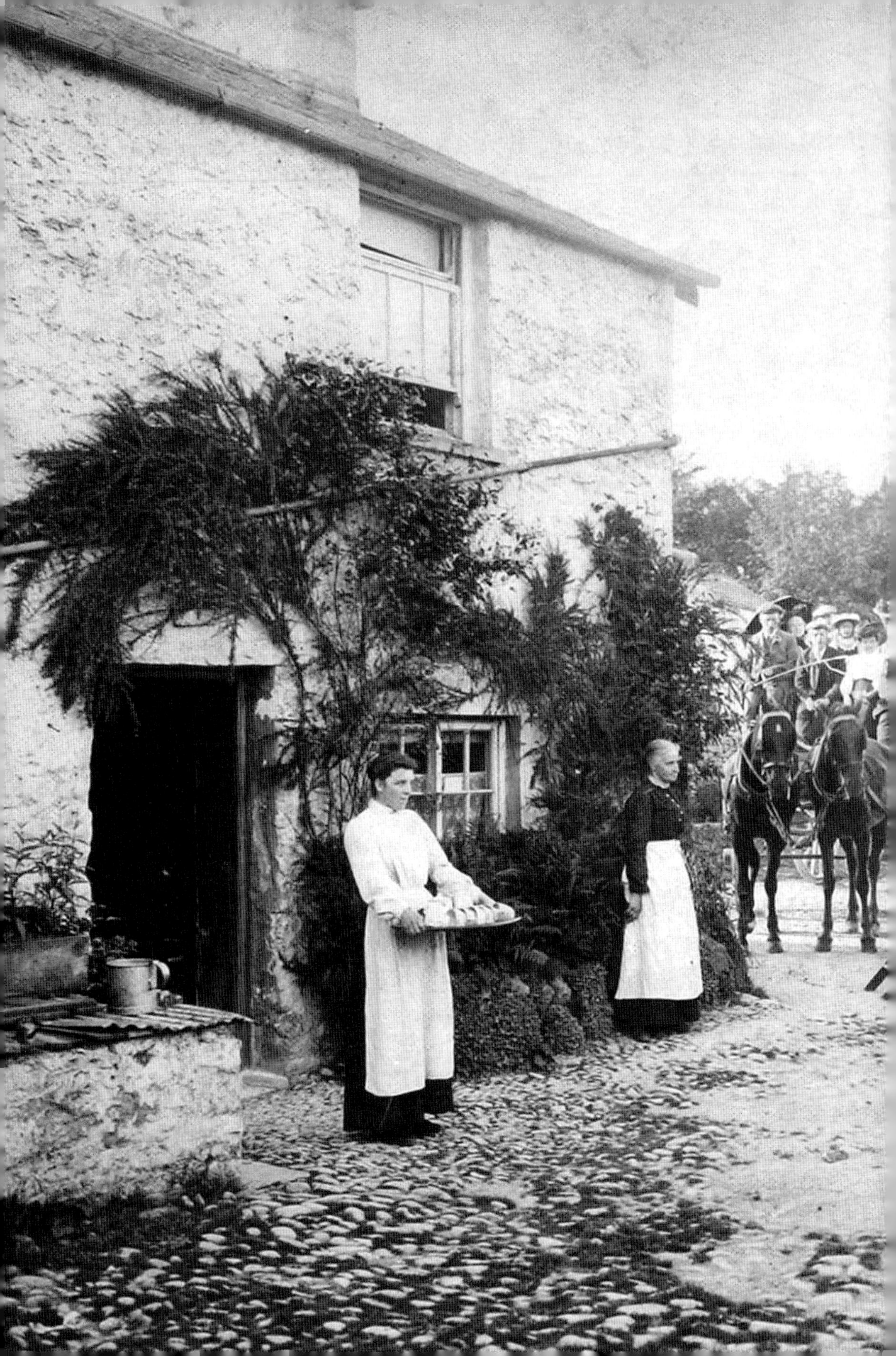

OLD SILVERDALE

The Loveliest Spot on Morecambe Bay

Rod J. Ireland

Dedicated to the late John Bolton

&

the people of Silverdale

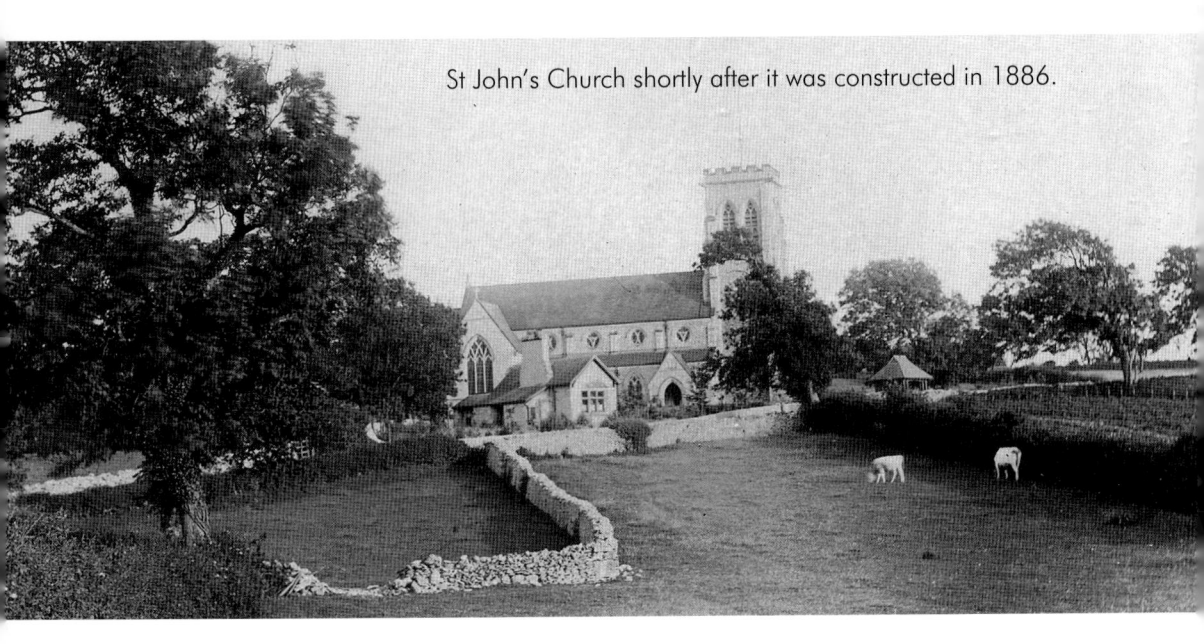

St John's Church shortly after it was constructed in 1886.

First published in 2016
by Palatine Books, Carnegie House, Chatsworth Road, Lancaster LA1 4SL
www.carnegiepublishing.com

Copyright © Rod J Ireland

All rights reserved
Unauthorised duplication contravenes existing laws

The right of Rod J Ireland to be identified as the author of this work has been asserted in
accordance with the Copyright, Designs and Patents Act 1988

British Library Cataloguing-in-Publication data
A catalogue record for this book is available from the British Library

Paperback ISBN 13: 978-1-910837-07-8

Designed and typeset by Carnegie Book Production

Printed and bound in Great Britain by TJ International Ltd, Padstow, Cornwall

CONTENTS

Introduction   1

1. *Ancient Silverdale*   4
2. *Growth of the Village*   8
3. *Grand Houses*   34
4. *Church and Chapel*   72
5. *Schooling*   91
6. *The Working Day*   104
7. *Life in the Village*   145
8. *Dark Days of War*   176
9. *Looking After the Visitors*   185

Acknowledgements   202

Silverdale Post Office with the windows full of picture postcards, many produced by Mr Lacy the village postmaster (c.1912).

INTRODUCTION

I FIRST CAME TO SILVERDALE IN 1950 on a seaside visit in my father's Triumph Renown. As a young man on a mission with a bucket and spade, I was more than a little disappointed to find that the 'sand' was about a mile from the shore. Thank goodness I continued to visit, for as I grew, my appreciation of the beauty of the area grew. As a young geologist I developed an understanding of the limestones that contributed greatly to the scenery. Numerous visits to this, the smallest Area of Outstanding Natural Beauty in the United Kingdom, turned my appreciation into affection.

Weekend leisure walks around the AONB became a regular feature of my life, but both my wife and myself had family and work commitments further south in Lancashire that frustrated our ambition to live here. As the Millennium approached our circumstances changed and we came to live on Cove Road in Silverdale.

I hadn't been in the village long when I picked up three old postcards in a saleroom. Very pleased with my find, I showed them to friends in the village. Soon I was asked if I was really interested in old postcards, a positive answer resulted in me being given a very large album of cards to peruse. This fired my enthusiasm and it was not long before I was privileged to attend one of John Bolton's old postcard slide shows in the Gaskell Hall. There I discovered that the album had been assembled by John Bolton and Margaret Pearson; I quickly realised that the two had gathered an amazing amount of local history to complement the cards.

History and photography are my favourite leisure interests, so I set off with great enthusiasm, to collect postcards. Almost immediately it became clear that I had 'missed the boat'. Cards were increasingly expensive and most of the rare ones had been snapped up years before. After some thought and advice from others, I came to the conclusion that I would be better employed photographing and scanning the images in order to assemble a village image archive in order to preserve these pictures in perpetuity.

Locals were very happy to loan me their treasured postcards and family photographs provided that they were treated with care and returned promptly. These same locals were keen to talk about the history of the images and I began to learn a little of the village history. This spurred me on to learn as much as I could about times gone by; I found the Mourholme Local History Society lectures and publications most helpful in this context. After several happy years scanning images and learning of local history, it was suggested by John Bolton that I may care to do a slide show in the Gaskell Hall. I was astounded at how well the event was supported. It resulted in me being invited to do slide shows elsewhere.

Meanwhile old age and infirmity led John Bolton to move to Grange over Sands. At this stage he indicated that he had made his contribution and it was over to me now. Next came suggestions that it would be good to produce a book of the best images with some historical background. This volume is the result, although it was the product of a rather long gestation period.

Probably the most difficult task in preparing this book has been the selection of images to be included. There were plenty to choose from. The archive now contains over a thousand images, postcards and photographs. We are particularly blessed with the number and variety of photographs, some early examples dating from the 1880s but most dating from the first two decades of the twentieth century.

With the new rail connection to the Leeds/Bradford cloth district, Silverdale became a destination for seaside holidays. Development of photography and a relaxation of postal regulations resulted in postcards becoming the preferred method of social communication. They were the text message of their time, over 16 million a year sent in the UK in the early 1900s. A card posted in Silverdale in the morning would be delivered in Bradford that afternoon.

There were a number of locally based photographers meeting the demand for postcards by holidaymakers and others. They included John and Jackson Taylor (Silverdale General Store/PO), J. E. Lacy (Silverdale Post Office), F. Crosland (Arnside), D. J. Wilson (Arnside Post Office) and Simco Ltd of Kendal. In addition there were a number of visiting photographers including Matthews of Bradford and Grayston Bird of Bath.

I must emphasise that it is contributions by the good people of Silverdale that have made this book possible. Their help came in many forms including a) a willingness to loan their own cards and photographs, b) the supply of historic data and information, c) their eagerness to identify individuals on photographs and d) suggestions as to where to look next. Any errors or omissions are entirely of my own making. Those who were particularly helpful are listed in the Acknowledgements. I would like to thank everyone in the village for their contributions. You have helped to make my task most pleasurable.

R. J. I.
Silverdale   August 2016

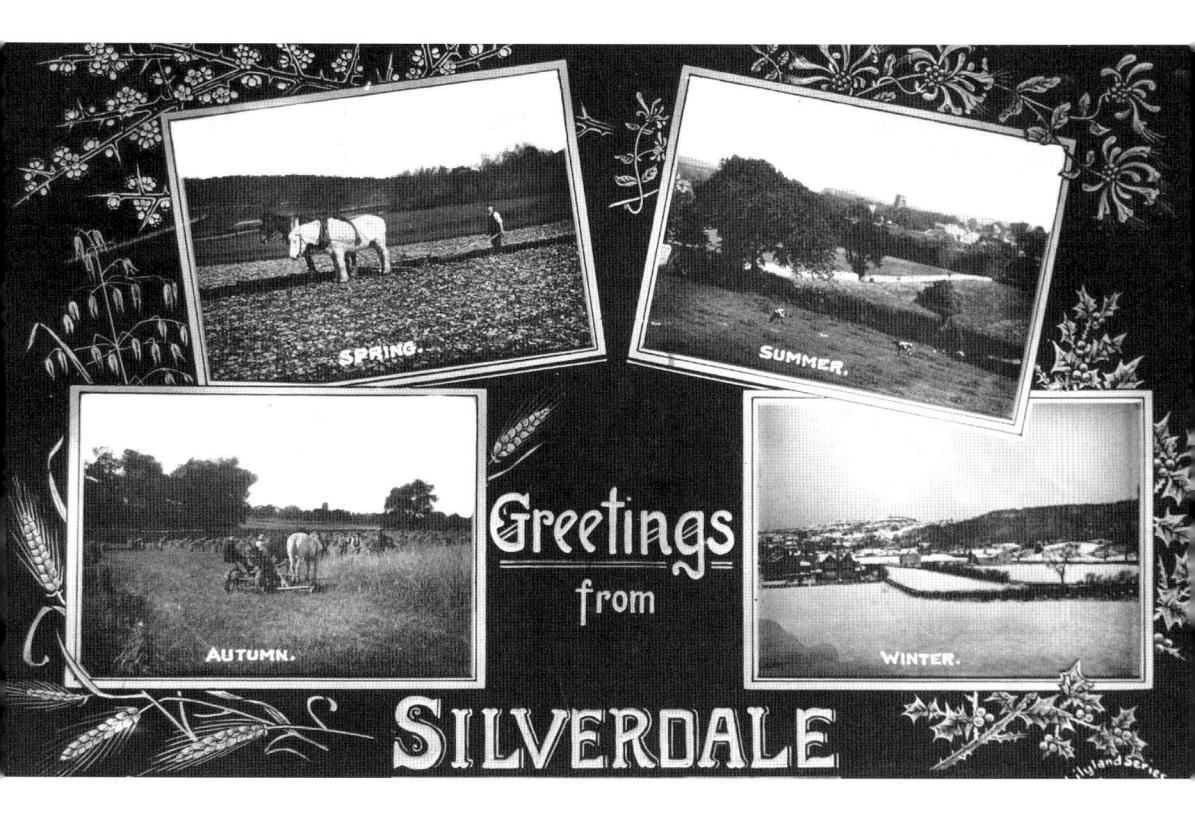

1

ANCIENT SILVERDALE

IN OLDEN TIMES before the coming of the railway, the township of Silverdale largely consisted of scattered farmsteads. There was no village centre as we know it today. Workers' cottages were clustered around the farms with small communities developing on the Green, The Row, Waterslack, Elmslack and the Cove. In addition, a small group of houses developed on Shore Road along the boundary of Silverdale and Lindeth townships.

Early farming would have been of the open field type practised in North Lancashire, but by the 1670s the best arable land had been enclosed under an award of the Silverdale Manor Court through the Lord of the Manor, Sir George Middleton of Leighton Hall. The enclosed land was split between 25 local landowners. The land was walled/fenced and gated. Outside the enclosure, the remaining land, known as 'the commons and waste', was used for grazing.

The gates were used to keep the grazing animals out of the enclosed arable areas in order to protect the crops during the growing season. After harvesting the gates were opened and the animals were allowed to graze on the enclosed land. Their dung provided an important natural fertiliser for the next year's crops.

Figure 1 shows the extent of the ancient enclosure. The old farms and their watering places are mostly located around the margins of the ancient enclosure, although the chapel of ease was conveniently located centrally within the township and the ancient enclosure.

Some of the ancient enclosure gate names have survived as road or house names, these include Emes Gate, Bradshaw Gate and Ford Gate. It is still possible to discern a large part of the ancient enclosure today. One of the best vantage points is the stile next to the Woodlands entrance off Park Road. From here one can see a large part of the more easterly section of the enclosure, still in agricultural use although most is now grazing rather that cultivated for crops.

The parish boundary was ridden or beaten at regular intervals by local groups of men and boys in order to ensure that there were no incursions by neighbouring parishes.

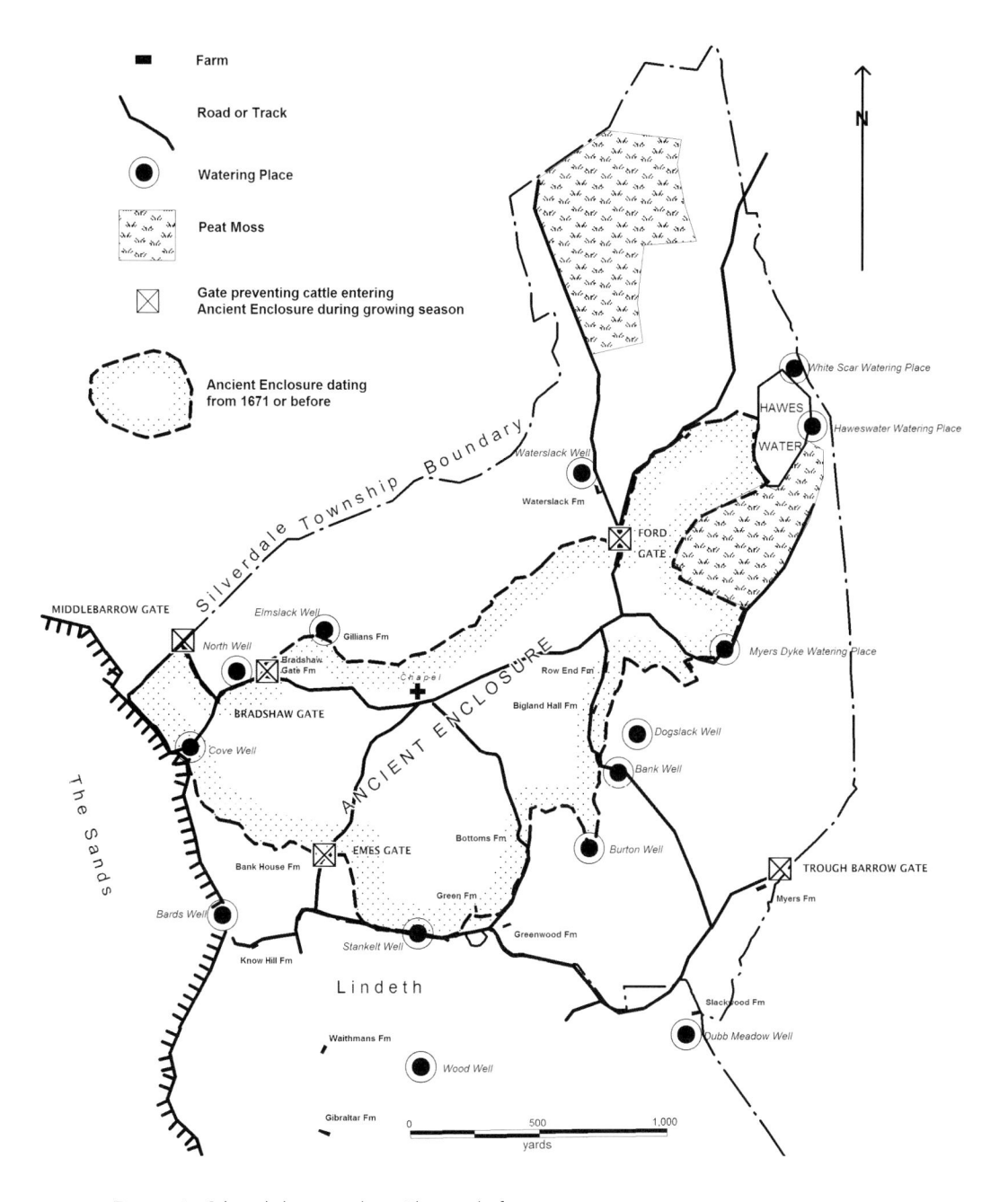

Figure 1: Silverdale township. The early farming community and the ancient enclosure from 1671 or before.

Riding or beating the bounds of Silverdale Parish. Here we see the local worthies assembling outside the Bath House, Shore Cottages, in 1895 to oversee those riding and walking the boundaries. Leaning in the window is James Rawlinson a retired fisherman, seated is Henry Thornton JP of Yew Tree House, Overseer of the Poor. Standing are Thomas Bolton (left) Surveyor of Highways, and James Hall the local builder, of Bank Villa.

The 1895 Silverdale boundary riding party assembled on the shore. The flag bearers were John Hall (left) and James Rawlinson. The young boys were there to learn the boundary route. Among them was a young Joe Bisbrown who was also present on the 1977 boundary beating seen below.

The 1977 party beating the bounds lead by Jim Bolton with sons Michael and David; others included a young Cedric Robinson, Juliet Turnbull and her mother Ann Turnbull on horseback, Ian Fogg, Stan Jenkins, and those carrying the inflatable are Robert Bolton, Bernard Fryer, Frank Holmes, Brian Dobson and Richard Proctor.

2

GROWTH OF THE VILLAGE

WEALTH GENERATED BY INDUSTRY, manufacture and shipping led to many of the early changes in the village. It is clear from the list of landowners in the Silverdale and Warton-with-Lindeth Enclosure Act (1811–17) allocations that the wealthy from elsewhere were investing in agricultural land and buildings as a source of income and pleasure. Owning land and forming country estates helped to increase the social standing of the new rich. The ownership of land was highly regarded and helped to establish one's place in society.

With land ownership came country residences. The first house built as a gentleman's seaside residence was Cove House, built by Rev. Carus Wilson, vicar of Tunstall and head of Cowan Bridge school for the daughters of the clergy. The original Cove House was built as a summer villa at the Cove in about 1810. He visited regularly and acquired several sections of adjacent coastline. During his time in Silverdale he generously supported the refurbishment of the church and on his death in 1859, he left his estate to his son-in-law Rev. Henry Shepheard who vigorously opposed the bay reclamation scheme and plans to take the Lancaster–Ulverston Railway along the shore. We owe a debt of gratitude to him for helping to keep the bay as it is today. More later on the reclamation scheme.

With the coming of the railway in 1857, Silverdale became so much more accessible to those in the industrial towns and cities of the North. The area provided opportunities for rural retreats far from the smoke and grime of the industrial centres, yet close enough to allow commuting to the factory, mill and office. The wealthy residents who had so strongly opposed the shore route for the Furness Railway became regular passengers once the line was constructed on the inland route.

The central section of this picture shows Rev. Carus Wilson's house 'The Cove' which is now incorporated into the present Abbeyfield Cove House (photo by Mr J. E. Lacy, the Silverdale Postmaster in the early 1920s). The section to the left of Carus Wilson's house was added by Henry Boddington, the Manchester brewer, when he extended and improved the whole building in 1879.

Another early gentleman's residence was initiated by Jackson Mason, a Lancaster solicitor descended from a local farming family. In 1800 he bought the Hill House estate. By 1808 he had sold the estate to Robert Inman, a Lancaster ship owner and merchant involved in the slave trade, who had inherited a fortune from his father Charles. In 1823 Robert died and the estate passed to his son Thomas Inman. It would appear that both Thomas and his father, whilst having a grand town house in Lancaster, enjoyed the prestige of a country estate but also regarded it as an investment in land. Inman left his mark in the Hill House estate with much landscaping, walling, tree planting and track building. Sadly there are no drawings or photos of Hill House other than a sketch of the house as shown on the Enclosure Award plan of 1817.

"The Cove", Silverdale

Silverdale station before 1909 (photo by Crosland of Arnside) with a passenger train bringing residents and trippers. Note the station cottages on the left and the Trowbarrow Lime Works chimney in the distance. Trowbarrow Quarry is to the right of the trees in the background. The station had its own signal box which is just visible at the far end of the opposite platform.

Henry Boddington, the Manchester brewer, was an early commuter. He had his own horse-drawn cab to take him from Cove House to the station, and pick him up on his return on the Manchester–Barrow train.

Silverdale station (about 1910) had staff including a stationmaster and porters. The station included sidings for loading goods such as fresh cockles, shrimps and fish bound for the cities. Note the large tank on the roof of the first building, which collected roof drainage. This was a common feature of village houses and provided the only source of domestic water until 1938 when mains water came to the area.

The station in the 1920s when there was a small shop, a slot machine for chocolate and a weighing machine under the veranda.

Silverdale signal box (1920) with signalman Robert Holden, grandfather of Angela Holden (née Chatburn).

Station staff (c.1920) including the Stationmaster Cecil Fitzjames, seated left.

The block of shops known as Holborn was built in the late 1890s and opened for business in January 1899. The first businesses were Armstrong's Confectioners, Fleming's Prize Boot Makers and Knight's the Butcher. Mr Fleming can be seen standing by his shop door watching the children. The photo must have been taken on some special occasion as the children appear to be dressed in their 'Sunday Best'. By 1902 Armstrong's had moved to what became Allendale Café on Stankelt Road and were replaced at No.1 Holborn by the Cunliffe family from Farnworth.

Reception Committee at Silverdale station (c.1910). On the left is Cecil Fitzjames, the stationmaster (1901 to 1929), centre Sergeant Pickup of Carnforth and right is Mr Morland, a porter/signalman.

Busy days in the village centre in the first decade of the 1900s with lots of holidaymakers and a new landlord at the Royal, Proctor Wilman. He took over from James Burrow in about 1902 but had left by 1907 when Thomas Grieg moved in, just in time for the coronation of George V.

The Royal in Wilman's time, taken about 1905. Proctor Wilman is standing in the front door, and John Fleming, the boot maker, is also standing in the shot dressed in his white apron. Cunliffe's of Farnworth were running the café at No. 1 Holborn.

In about 1907 Thomas C. Greig took over as tenant of the Royal. His name is writ large on the main hotel sign. Within two years he had erected a verandah across the front, mentioned in the 1909 valuation. In the same period a verandah was built onto the front of the café. Cunliffe's sign has disappeared and been replaced with a Hovis advert. To the right of the butcher's is the field on which the Gaskell Hall was built.

The landlord introduced an early form of 'café society' to the village. During his thirty years in the Royal, Greig did much to promote trade and hosted a variety of activities.

Advertising obviously pays off! A large group of ladies dressed in their best, taking tea. The large script suggests that this postcard was also used for advertising.

A postcard clearly designed as an advert. The reality is that the group is posed. Seated on the right is Thomas Greig himself, while his family make up the rest of the group.

The Royal hosted meetings of The Oddfellows and the Royal Ancient Antediluvian, Order of Buffaloes. Here we see a group of Oddfellows with Greig in shirt sleeves standing at the back.

This is one of the most revealing images of the village centre. Dating from about 1930 it shows that Greig had left the Royal, and the RAOB was still meeting in the hotel. Brock's pharmacy was located on the corner of what is now Gaskell Close. At this time the Close was occupied by 'Westfield Public Putting Green', 18 holes and 3 old pence per round. Fresh fish was for sale down at the Putting Green. The café had become the Holborn Café. To the right of the butcher's is a drystone wall with a white notice. Careful examination shows that it announced that this was to be the 'Site of the Gaskell Memorial Village Hall'. Sadly it's not possible to read the smaller writing on the lower part of the board; however it is likely to have been an appeal for donations. I was told by a villager who was a young girl at this time that there was, through the stile just visible behind the two ladies, a collection box on a ledge in the wall. What honest times!

The severe winter of 1962. Snow on the ground in the village. The phone box is new, together with a strange square brick building on the Royal car park. It is rumoured that it had been an air raid shelter!

Emesgate in 2006 with the Royal open for business. Note that the verandah has been glazed to form an extra room.

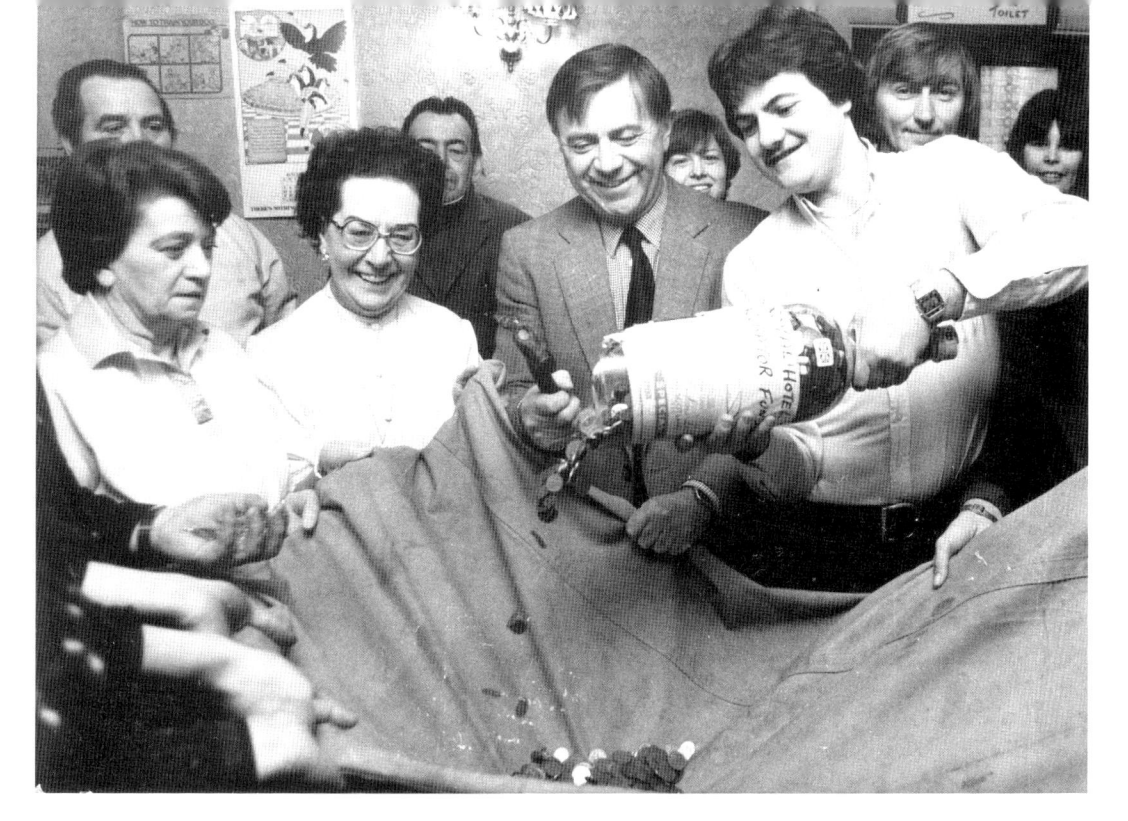

Happy times in the Royal bar, where George Turnbull breaks the 'penny bottle' to collect the donations for an incubator at the maternity unit where he was the consultant gynecologist and obstetrician.

Emesgate before the Gaskell Hall, which was built in 1931. On the left is the arched doorway that forms the entrance to the library. To the right is Laburnum House, the left-hand side of which was the bank (1908–90) in what is now the doctor's surgery. The pharmacy on the right was a general store, run for many years by the Cooke family.

A deserted view of the village centre with the Post Office on the left. For many years the postmaster was Mr J. E. Lacey. He took some of the best early photographs of the village and sold them as postcards. In the early 1900s cards posted in the morning would be delivered that same afternoon, even as far away as Bradford!

Looking down Emesgate towards Stankelt Road we see Wilkinson's Chemists shop (later Buck's) and the Ambrose Café with its outside seating area. Further down the road the ground floor of Stankeld House (formerly Victoria Bank) had been converted into a shop. For a time the post office moved to these premises but then moved back to its former location.

After the Post Office moved back to its previous location, the premises were converted into a café known as the 'Coffee Bar'. On the left is Mrs Crabtree, the owner, with her helper, a young Carole Waddington.

The Coffee Bar became a magnet for the young people of the area as demonstrated by lots of familiar faces in this 1960s photo on the right.

Stankelt Road. This was the first property built in Silverdale by R. J. Bolton, builder, for his own family. The Bolton family came to live in the right-hand house, known as Meadow Bank, and rented out the next door draper's shop, Regent House, to Agnes Robinson of the Robinson family of Hazelwood Farm. At the front of Meadow Bank are Mrs R. J. Bolton and sons Wilf and Tom.

When the Boltons moved to Croftlands by the shore, Meadow Bank was converted to a shop with an extension to the right. It was known as Gardner's General Stores and run by Cyril and Lily Farrer (above left and right). The extension housed a greengrocer's and fish shop; the store was later run by W. & M. Turner. Finally Phil Ashworth had a small electrical store here before the building was converted to two dwellings with an extra floor added on the single storey extension.

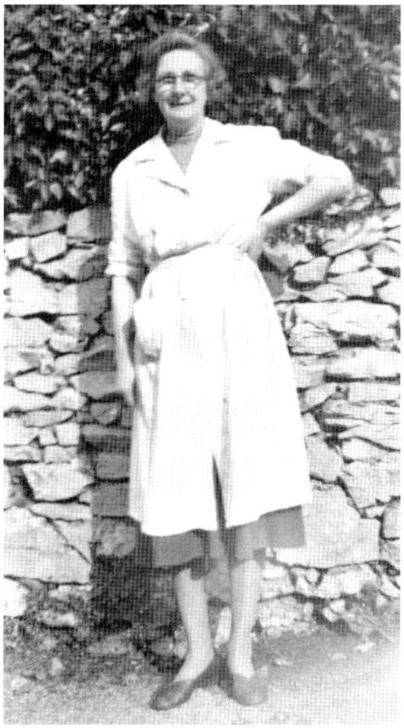

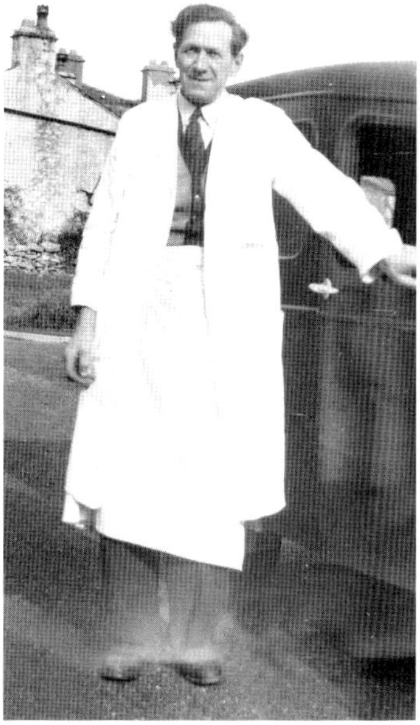

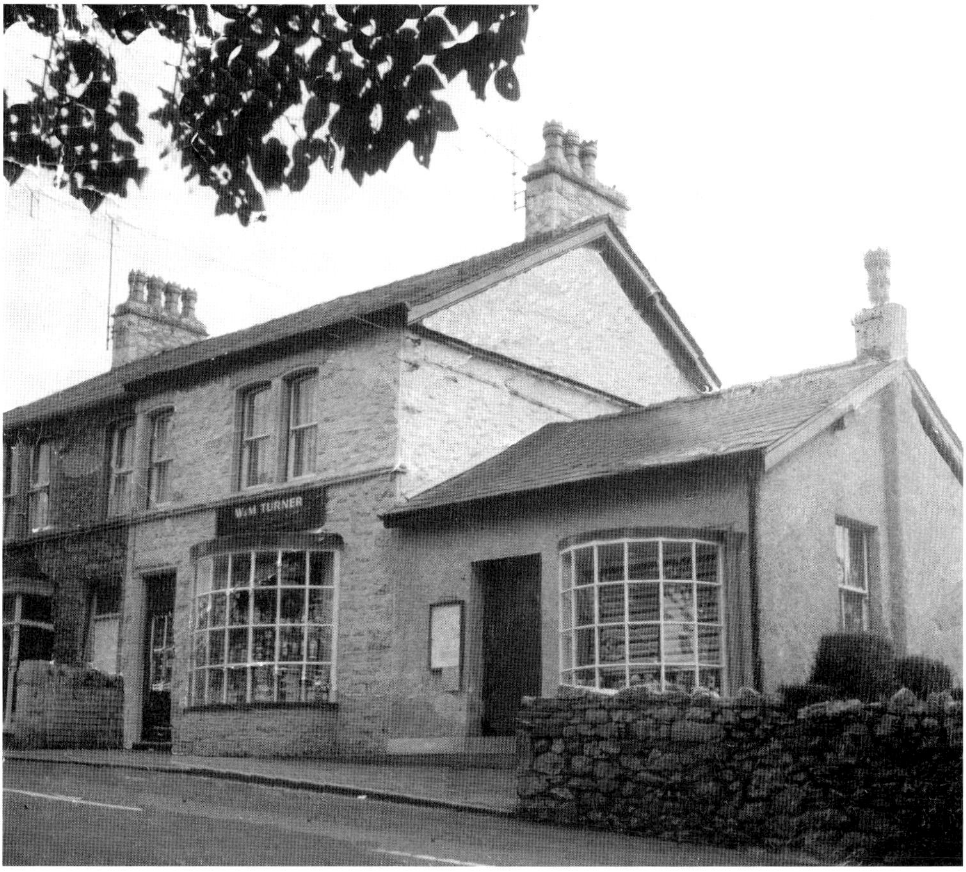
W&M TURNER

Next door to the Nook on Stankelt Road was Richmond's Boot & Shoe shop and Newsagents. Judging from the news on the boards, the photo was probably taken about 1906. As business grew, the boot and shoe sales moved across the road to a corrugated iron building on the site now occupied by the flats between Regent House and Allendale Cafe. This can be seen on several old photos of Stankelt Road.

This view down Stankelt Road (c.1910) shows Richmond's Boot & Shoe shop in the corrugated iron building directly opposite the newsagents.

The Armstrong family of No.1 Holborn moved here to the shop and café built for them by R. J. Bolton in 1902. During its time the building has been the British Legion, Silverdale Social Club, a fish and chip shop and the Allendale Café. The business was run for many years by the Dolden family. The building is now a domestic dwelling but the name board is still to be seen over the downstairs window to the right of the entrance in this photo.

In 1907 the Institute, designed by the famous Lancaster architects Paley & Austin, was opened along Spring Bank (Barkers Lane). At the time there was great enthusiasm locally for the provision of a place where people, particularly the young, could gather to take recreation and instruction without the distractions of politics, sectarianism or alcohol.

At Rock House at the Green, John Carr (proprietor) was offering a variety of services including 'Livery Stables, Carriages for Hire, Luggage Removed, Ducklings for Sale (dressed to order), Refreshments, Mineral Waters and Accommodation'. His brother Robert was farming at the Green and John is here photographed with his brother's children in about 1900.

Until 1931 the Parish Rooms were next to the old Chapel at the junction of Cove Road, Emesgate and Park Road. The rear of the building was the Tithe Barn. After the Tithe Commutation Act the building was used as a school and was enlarged in 1855 and 1878. After the new school was built in 1896 it became the Parish Rooms until 1931. It was the home of the Silverdale Village Players but it quickly became clear that it was too small to stage full productions, so the Players gave their support to a plan to build a new village hall. Both the Parish Rooms and the old Chapel were converted to dwelling houses in the 1980s.

In about 1900 Mr Knight the butcher would have been a familiar sight around the village as he delivered meat to his customers.

James Burrow took over the butcher's shop about 1911. During the early 1900s he gradually aquired the whole of Holborn. He left the Royal and started a butchery business which is still operated by the Burrows family today. James and his wife Sarah Thwaite were the first couple to be married in the new St John's Church. While they were at the Royal, seven of their eight children were born, including two sets of twins in 1897 and 1898 (see next page).

William Henry (Harry), Frederick Jubilee and Victor Jubilee (twins born in Jubilee year 1897), Stanley Airey and Harvey Thwaite (twins born in 1898), James and Margaret.

The two sets of twins were born less than eleven months apart, one set in August 1897 and the other in June 1898. At the Royal Hotel, postcards showing the four boys were sold to the tourists. The local men used to put pennies down the backs of the twins' clothing. A man who worked for the family used to push the four babies around the village in a wheelbarrow.

Harvey was always regarded as being delicate and his twin brother was very protective towards him. When Harvey was called up to go into the army first, Stanley offered to go in his place. Ironically, the delicate Harvey outlived all his brothers by several years.

The Gaskell Memorial Hall, Silverdale.

In 1928 the fire at the parish rooms precipitated moves to build a bigger and better village hall. Donations came in from everywhere. Sir Norman Rae of Harrogate gave £100 on the understanding that it be called Gaskell Memorial Hall. The largest donation came from F. J. Dickens of the Woodlands. Herbert Bright of Cove House donated land from the Bank House Farm Estate. Building costs were £3000 and the hall was opened by Mrs Bright on 6 February 1931. Lighting used electricity from Bradford Dyers Association's own generator next door at Bleasdale.

Going down Emesgate we come to what is now known as The Old Forge Cottage. Here we see John Fleming, the boot and shoe maker, in his Tam o' Shanter, standing outside his shop. Sometime after 1911 he left Holborn and moved to these new premises. He was a colourful character, a Cumberland/Westmorland wrestler who liked a drink. When he married Elinor Walker from Waterslack he gave up the drink and became a Salvationist. The lamp on the corner incorporated a sign saying 'God is Love'. He was known to berate the vicar when he passed, exclaiming 'St John's Church would never be a success as it was built with beer money from Boddington'. How wrong he was!

Another view of The Old Forge, probably taken on the same occasion as the previous one, given that John Fleming is wearing the same clothes but this time joined by companions. He was renowned for spinning many a good tale or waxing lyrical on any topic, usually at the expense of his work. The ground floor was the business premises and upstairs was the living accommodation reached by the external stairway. The corrugated tank standing by the steps collected roof drainage and was the only source of supply till piped water arrived in 1938. On the left of the card is The Cabin, a small shop run by Miss Hurst. It was said that this was like Aladdin's Cave and that you could buy anything here! Behind The Cabin in the dark shed and the building beyond was Mr T. Robinson's stables, livery and smithy. He had a fine fleet of carriages and one of the first cars in the village, known as Big Bertha. In addition he kept donkeys and operated rides on the beach.

The Old Forge had several uses after the Flemings were there, including as Dyson's Fish and Chip shop, which closed in WWII due to a shortage of dripping. In 1970 Mrs Dorothy Brown bought the property and opened Tara Antiques; here she is sitting outside the shop. In addition her son, Tony, opened a private restaurant upstairs, and he is seen below in his chef's whites catering for a wedding party. It is rumoured that restaurant was once patronised by Royalty!

By the 1920s there were 14 shops in the village, 11 farms delivering milk and 9 travelling traders calling regularly. Here is one of the travelling traders at the toll house on the junction of Sand Lane and New Road on the Silverdale to Warton Turnpike road.

The New Road along the foot of Warton Crag remained a Turnpike Toll Road until May 1927. This large group is gathered at Warton Toll House to celebrate the opening of the road in 1927. The toll house was subsequently demolished and all that remains today is a small area of open land where Sand Lane residents park cars.

Silverdale level crossing keeper's house, which was demolished when a continental crossing was put in during the 1960s. Crossing keeper for many years was George Hodkinson. Other keepers were Thomas Burrows, Harry I'anson and George Taylor. The house was also used as a shop and general store.

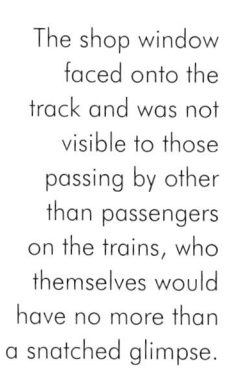

The shop window faced onto the track and was not visible to those passing by other than passengers on the trains, who themselves would have no more than a snatched glimpse.

3

GRAND HOUSES

Cove House. The central section of Cove House was built by the Rev. William Carus Wilson in 1820. This sketch is taken from the sales catalogue of 1876 when Henry Boddington, of the Manchester Brewery, bought the place and constructed the left-hand section of the house shown on the postcard opposite.

Here on the left we see the Boddington addition to the house, the right-hand section being the original Carus Wilson house. The photo was taken in the early 1950s before a flat-roofed section was added on the right-hand side by the Stonebower Fellowship.

In about 1860 Henry Boddington bought a cottage at this site and used it for holidays. When later he bought Cove House he had the Oratory built. It was demolished by the Stonebower Trust after they bought Cove House in 1951.

An aerial view of Cove House before 1950. The Oratory can be seen in the trees to the left of the main house. The picture was taken before Stonebower added the flat-roofed extension on the right of the main house. Cove Lea, the kitchen gardens and staff housing can be clearly seen. By the time the property was sold in 1905 it included most of the coastal strip between the county boundary and Shore Road, including Bank House Farm.

Below left: Reverend William Carus Wilson who built Cove House in the 1820s. Apart from his association with the Brontë girls, who attended one of his schools, he will also be remembered as founder of the first penny periodical *The Children's Friend* magazine.

This page: Major George Morley Saunders, the third owner 1905–18, with his son.

Major Morley Saunders employed a large staff at Cove House. The chauffeur, Mr Nelson, is on the left, and Mr Newman, the head gardener, is on the extreme right.

Cove House greenhouse (c.1910), with Yorkie Richmond, Mr Newman and Dick Moss. The under gardener Dick died in WWI a few short years after this photo was taken. His death in 1917 is, today, remembered on the Silverdale War Memorial.

Outside their home, Cove Lodge, in 1903 we see Mr Newman the head gardener with his wife, and daughter Daphne accompanied by her guinea pig. Nine years later in 1912 Daphne was crowned Empire Day Queen.

In 1920 Cove House was bought by Herbert Bright, cousin of John Bright the cotton baron and social reformer. Rumour has it that Herbert Bright searched for a country residence for some time. Dejected at his lack of success he was on the point of giving up when he visited Cove House, saw the initials HB and took this as a good omen. The Brights established an internationally famous polo pony stud on the Lots. Here we see Mr and Mrs Herbert Bright receiving a Pony Club prize from Prince Arthur of Connaught in 1928.

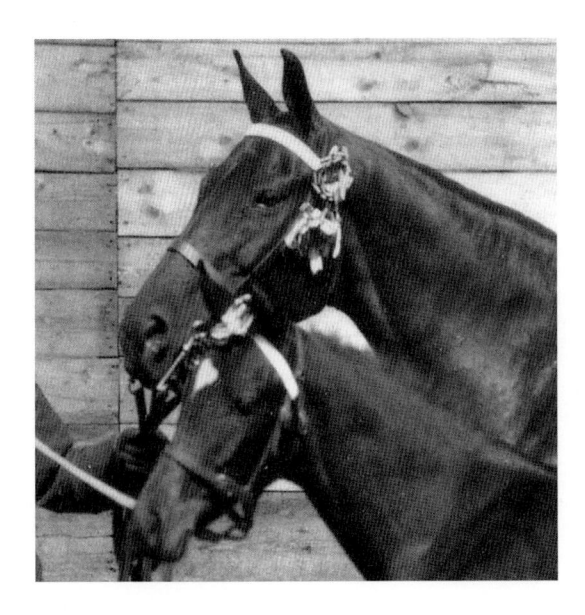

Opposite and left: Silvery II and foal Tabitha at the Royal Show Harrogate in 1929, held by Dick Mason, the Brights' groom, from Bank House Farm. Silvery II was shown six times at Royal Shows and won 1st twice and 2nd four times, all helping to give Silverdale Polo Pony Stud its well-deserved reputation.

Assembled on the Lots are the 1937 Royal Show winners, gold, silver and bronze. This photo was used on the Bright family calendar (1938).

MARCH 2nd and 3rd, 1928.

SILVERDALE 19.

THE COVE,
SILVERDALE,
NR. CARNFORTH.

MR. HERBERT BRIGHT'S PONIES.

NATIONAL PONY SHOW PRIZE WINNERS.

As reported in last Saturday's "Rochdale Observer," Mr. Herbert Bright won both the senior and junior polo pony championships and was also successful in the mares' produce class at the National Pony Show opened in London on Friday last. The show was continued on Saturday, when Mr. Bright was again one of the prize-winners. Details of his awards are as follows:—

Open stallion class.—First prize, gold medal, special for best polo bred stallion, champion cup, and also reserve for the trophy.

Colts up to three years old.—First prize, gold medal, challenge cup, & reserve for same.

Yearling colts.—Third prize.

Two years old colts.—First prize.

Three years old colts.—1st and 2nd prizes.

Three years old fillies.—2nd prize & reserve.

Two and three years old geldings—1st prize.

Open stallions.—First and reserve.

Polo bred stallion.—First prize.

Dam's produce.—First and gold medal.

Sire's produce.—First and gold medal.

Last year Mr. Bright also won in both the produce classes, which are very important to breeders.

The challenge cups won this year were presented to Mr. Bright by Princess Arthur of Connaught.

Herbert Bright (centre) receiving two young Princesses at the National Pony Society Annual Show in London in 1937. Mr Bright gave the land for the Gaskell Hall and Lovelight Alley in 1931. His son Tom gave Bank House Farm to the National Trust in 1983.

Cove Lea on Cove Lane (1906), leading down to the shore, was the home of Mrs Bright after the death of her husband in 1950. In recent years it was, for a time, the home of Victoria Wood.

The Peace Pledge Union (a pacifist group closely allied with the Quakers) was fired with a desire to help old people living in difficult conditions – some were living in air raid shelters or old tunnels, having been bombed out of their houses. Fred Helliwell of Hest Bank, one of the founders, opened a house at Burton in Lonsdale. It was run on a shoestring but supported by donations. It also provided employment for conscientious objectors.

Stonebower Fellowship, Silverdale

In 1949 the Stonebower Fellowship was incorporated into the Housing Society Ltd. In 1950 when Cove House became available, the Stonebower Fellowship bought it. LCC donated £1000 on the condition that at least 10 residents would be from Lancashire. Help came from the Nuffield Corporation and the National Association for Care of Old People. In 1951 the chairman Charles Wade went on the BBC Home Service programme, 'This Week's Good Cause' (5 August). This raised £1000. Shortly afterwards Stonebower moved to Cove House and by 1954 they had 28 residents. The decision was taken in the 1980s to donate the whole estate to Silverdale Abbeyfield Society, with whom it now rests.

Bleasdale. The house was built in 1860 for Nathaniel Wordsall, a railway wagon builder of Crewe, who named it Delamere Cottage. Note the spire on the turret at the corner of the house. The house changed hands several times before being occupied by a noted rose grower, J. T. Marsden, the Manchester colliery owner.

This is probably how the house looked in 1903 when Toby and Pearl Sharp bought it for £1800. In 1911 Pearl and Toby had substantial alterations made to the house and renamed it Bleasdale, after a house they had once owned to the south of Lancaster.

In 1911 the Sharps also had the coach house, stables, garage and billiard room built on the opposite side of Emesgate Lane. The work was carried out by Riggs of Carnforth.

THE GARAGE BLEASDALE HOUSE SILVERDALE

The main entrance was improved and the spire was removed from the top of the turret. The Sharps only stayed two or three years before they moved to Hazelwood. The Sharps brought their staff with them and introduced some new surnames to the village; these included Housley, Raisbeck, Lockwood, Lucas and Marriner.

This aerial shot of Bleasdale shows the extent of the gardens to the front of the main house, the scale of the coach house, and the kitchen gardens to the right of the coach house. The Sharps bought Oak Lea next door (now Cumbria View) in 1909 and developed the kitchen gardens on land belonging to Oak Lea but on the opposite side of Emesgate Lane. Part of this land is now home to the village fire station.

With the outbreak of war in 1914 the Sharps offered Bleasdale for use as a Voluntary Aid Detachment (VAD) hospital for wounded servicemen (August 1916 to February 1919). It was largely staffed by local volunteers from all sections of the village. Dr Jackson of Carnforth was the Medical Officer and was assisted by three trained nurses, two of whom can be seen on this photograph taken in 1916.

When it first opened the VAD had twenty beds, but by 1917 this had doubled to forty beds. This photo (1918) shows the staff and the injured soldiers in their hospital uniforms and was taken in Bleasdale House grounds.

One of the wounded soldiers, William Brabben, in a VAD ward. In its three years as a hospital some 280 wounded soldiers were treated and none was lost; a great achievement for the forty local volunteers and medical staff.

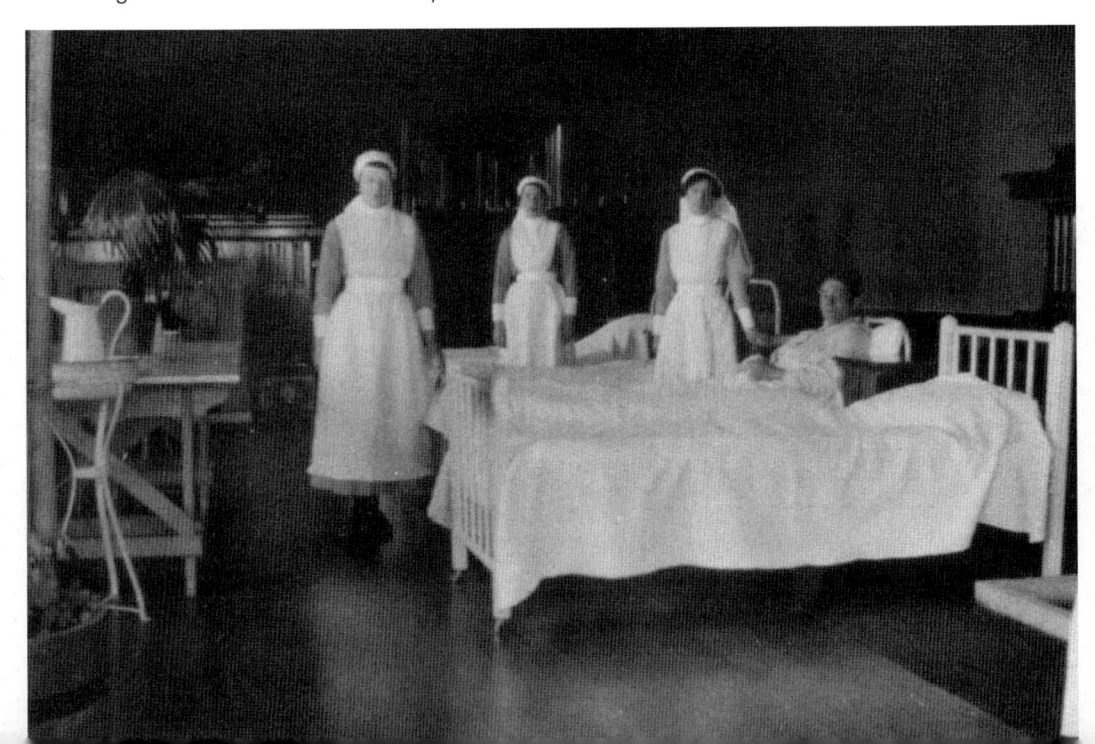

In 1914 the Sharps moved on to Hazelwood and never returned to Bleasdale. They sold it to the Bradford Dyers Association (BDA) and it became a convalescent home for employees, particularly those returning from the war. Here in 1930 we see the bowling green that was created on the front lawn. The BDA made the home into a war memorial to remember their 707 employees killed in the war and 37 workers killed in the disastrous Low Moor munitions factory explosion of 1916.

The BDA formal gardens in 1938. In 1948 Lancashire County Council bought Bleasdale to be used as a special school.

The Bleasdale head gardener, Mr Robert Raisbeck, and his wife in one of the kitchen garden greenhouses. Mr Raisbeck came to Silverdale to plan new gardens for the Sharps; he lived at Rose Cottage next to the fire station on Emesgate Lane.

Gardeners working on main house gardens in 1950. At the back are Bill Atkinson and Fred Wilson. Kneeling in the foreground is Eddie Glover who had been the village postman up to WWII.

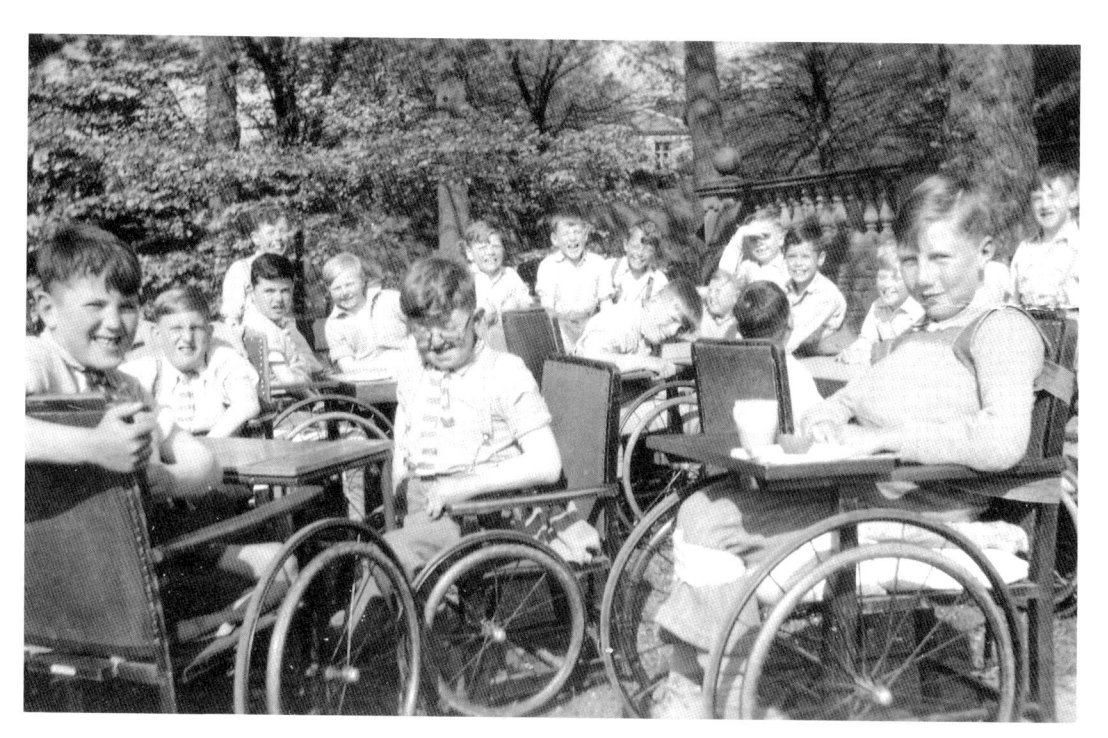

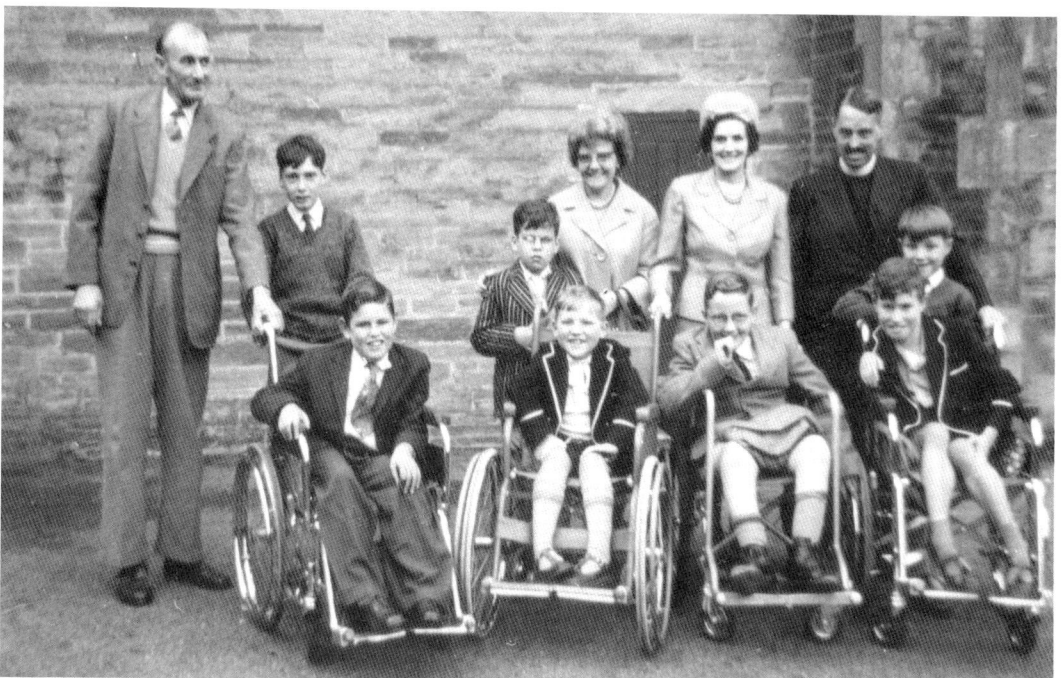

Top: In the early days of the special school the residents were mostly children who had suffered polio. Here are some of them out in the grounds on a sunny day (1950)

Above: Eddie Glover and his two sons Stuart and Paul taking some of the children to the Methodist Church for the Sunday service in 1950.

The special school kitchen staff, from left to right, Phyllis Housley, Rose Pearson, Florence (Hendy) Henderson and Winifred Edgar.

The nursing staff at the special school in 1949 having a well-earned break with tea and biscuits.

THE MOUNTAIN VIEW HOTEL, SILVERDALE.   24651

Oak Lea was built in 1866 for Nathaniel Radford. In 1909 the Sharp family from next door bought it and changed the name to Mountain View. The Champion family rented it for several years before it was converted to a hotel after WWII and run by Mr and Mrs Schofield. In the 1980s it was opened as a residential home under the direction of Mrs Marie Motch. Later, the home closed and the building is now an annex to a boys' school at Halecat.

View from the Mountain View Hotel with Castlebarrow in the foreground and Arnside Knott in the distance. Willy Riley's Windyridge is just right of centre, and Broomfield, with its bedroom windows peeping over the spite wall, is below and to the right of Windyridge.

Woodlands. An early picture of the house before there was any building on this section of Cove Road. The land was bought by Robert Inman, a ship owner of Lancaster in 1808. In 1811 his son Thomas had Hill House built on the site of two cottages. He undertook tree planting, road building and enclosure, and ran the estate as a business operation. He is remembered today by Inman's Road, a track leading from the Woodlands to Waterslack Farm, as seen on OS maps. He built many walls to enclose the commons and wastes allocated to him under the Enclosure Act 1811–17.

In 1858 the estate was bought by Christopher Wood, a master calico printer and mill owner of Brinscall. Within a year he had knocked down Hill House and replaced it with the present building, the Woodlands, designed by architect Thomas Birtwistle of Blackburn. No expense was spared and a new date stone for 1858 was included to signify the change of name to the Woodlands, thus incorporating the Wood name for posterity. Mr Wood brought his gardener, Edward Ireland, to design and manage his formal gardens.

In 1873 the Woodlands was sold to John Hebden, a cotton spinner from Vernon Mill, Bolton. Both he and his wife were Wesleyan Methodists and are fondly remembered for their help in establishing the Methodist church in Silverdale. Initially the Hebdens made an outbuilding at the Woodlands available for meetings before the church was built on Cove Road in 1879. After Mr Hebden died in 1889 his widow stayed on at the Woodlands till 1905. The first Methodist meetings were held in the building to the left of the main house as seen on the above pre 1911 photograph.

Henry Pratt, a soap and dolly blue manufacturer of Dukinfield, lived here from 1905 to 1916. Between 1916 and 1942 F. J. Dickens, a Manchester banker and cotton merchant, was the owner. He supported the Silverdale Village Players and promoted the building of the Gaskell Hall as their new home after a fire at the Parish Rooms, and he gave Eaves Wood to the National Trust. In Dickens' time the house reverted to its original name 'Hill House'.

Robert Inman, who bought Hill House in 1808. His son Thomas later took over until 1858.

Christopher Wood (1858–73)

Mr Pratt (1905–16), standing at his gate.

F. W. Dickens, who came in 1916 till 1942.

In 1905 the property was purchased for a total of £8050 by Henry Pratt, the first mayor of Dukinfield, and the manufacturer of Compo Washing Powder. He did much to encourage social activities in the village. He allowed the fields in front of the house to be used for sports, fetes and maypoles, etc. This area is now Clevelands Avenue! He championed the building of the Institute as a venue free of politics, religion and alcohol for the young men of the village, and was one of the first trustees.

Between 1916 and 1942 the Woodlands was owned by Mr F. J. Dickens, a banker and cotton merchant. During his time he helped to raise funds for the building of Gaskell Hall and was most supportive of the Silverdale Village Players. Later he gave Eaves Wood to the National Trust. After Dickens the Woodlands became a hotel and the National Trust acquired the balance of the woodland up to the county boundary.

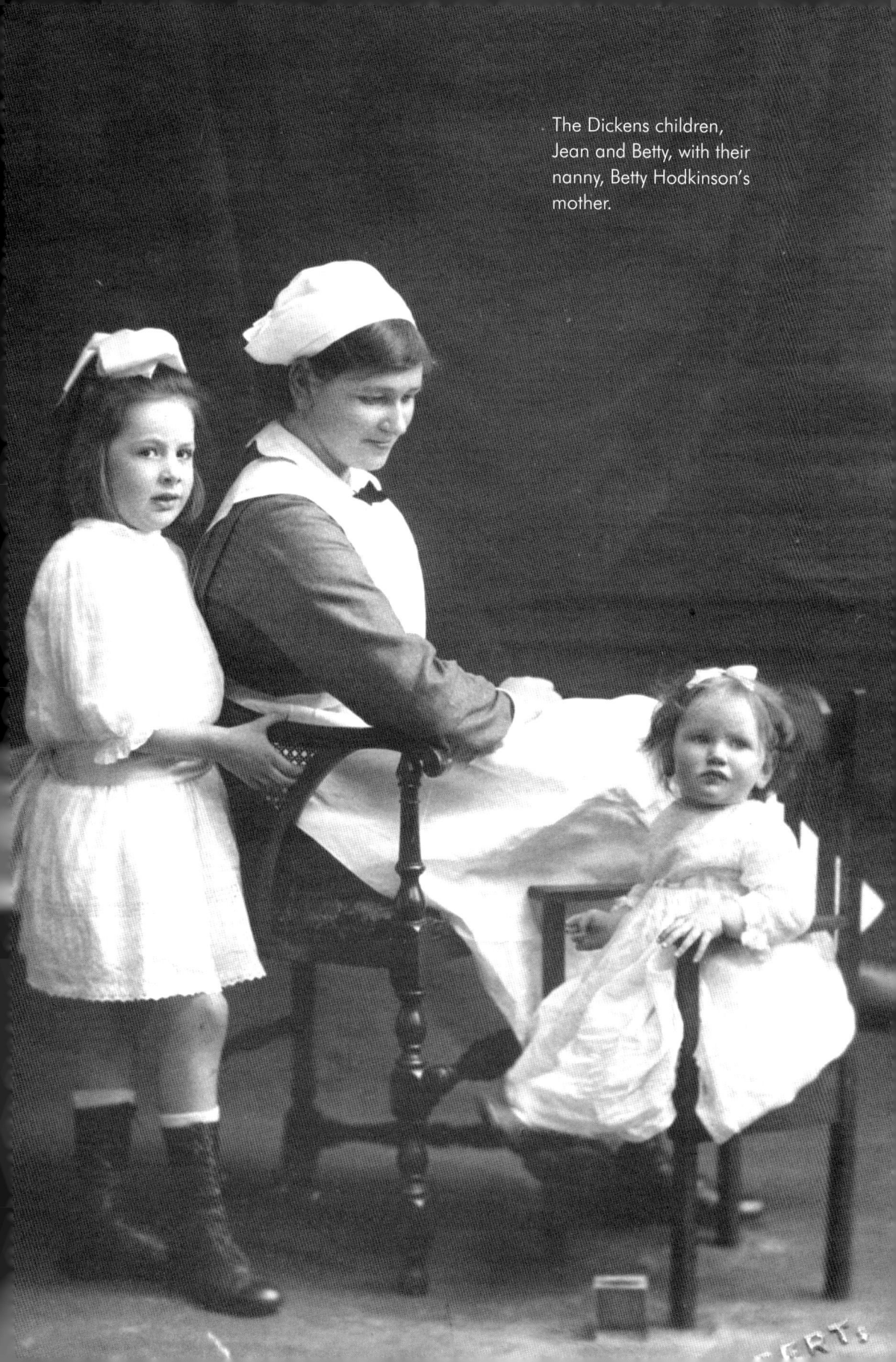

The Dickens children, Jean and Betty, with their nanny, Betty Hodkinson's mother.

The Woodlands' gardens in 1905, when Mr Pratt moved in.

The Woodlands from Emesgate Lane in about 1905 (Crosland of Arnside). The field in front of the Woodlands was for many years used for village events.

Maypole on the Woodlands Field on Empire Day in 1912.

Preparations for Mrs Calvert's Field Day June 1930 under Mrs Calvert's supervision. She lived at West Lindeth, and was the widow of a noted solicitor from Leigh, and a well-loved benefactor to the village school children.

Mrs Calvert's Field Day on 7 June 1930 with the children enjoying 'Punch & Judy' in the Woodlands Field.

Hazelwood, built on the site of Hill Top Farm by Leonard Willan in the early 1840s, was a private dwelling. Toby and Pearl Sharp had not settled in Bleasdale and they bought Hazelwood in about 1913. This postcard shows the house very much as it was when the Sharps acquired it.

"HAZELWOOD" SILVERDALE.

Before the Sharps moved in, a children's sports day and flower show were held on the main lawn in front of the house in 1912. In 1913 as soon as Pearl moved in, she commissioned the renowned architect Thomas Mawson to design new terracing and remodel the main reception rooms.

The new veranda and terracing on the west elevation of the main house as designed by Thomas Mawson of the E. Prentice Mawson practice.

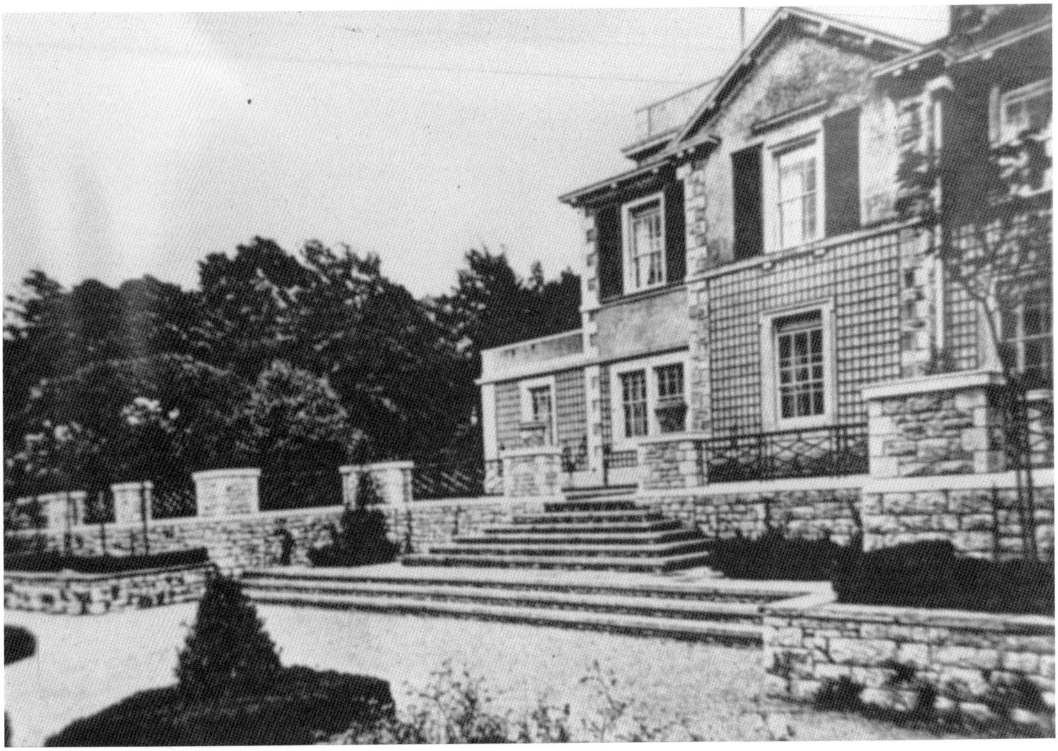

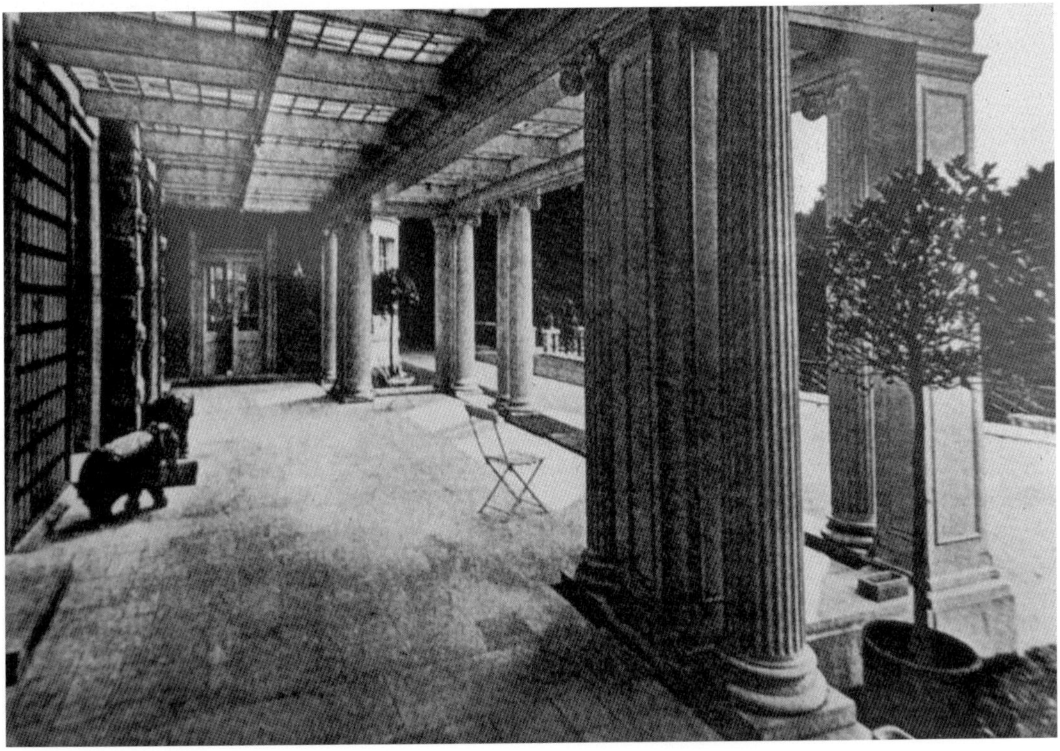

MODERN DOMESTIC ARCHITECTURE (SERIES II.). XLIV. – THE DINING-ROOM, "HAZELWOOD," SILVERDALE.
E. PRENTICE MAWSON, ARCHITECT.

The approach to the main entrance on the north elevation was also remodelled.

Under the veranda on the west elevation.

St. John of God Hospital and Noviciate, Silverdale 2531

Within 5 years of completion of the works, Pearl decided to move to Kent and rented the house to Harold Carrington of Carrington Dewhurst. The Carrington family finally bought Hazelwood in 1945. After Harold's death his widow bequeathed the house to the Roman Catholic Church. It became St John of God Hospital. It was later sold and became a residential home before being converted into apartments.

Opposite: two photographs of West Lindeth. Formerly known as Hole House, the house was built in 1780 but had later additions and alterations. In the 1870s the house was acquired by Herbert J. Walduck, a mining agent, owner and promoter. It was Walduck who set about obtaining parliamentary powers to reclaim the bay for agricultural use. Fortunately lack of finance and a number of catastrophes brought the scheme to a premature conclusion before the bay was damaged beyond repair. By 1891 Walduck had sold the house and was renting the Hermitage on Stankelt Road.

In 1919 West Lindeth was bought by Miss Ward and she married Mr Calvert, a highly regarded solicitor from Leigh. Mrs Calvert was remembered for the Christmas Tea she provided each year for the village school children. She also organised a summer Field Day for the children. Their name also survives with the Calvert Cup, which Mr and Mrs Calvert donated to the Silverdale Bowling Club.

WEST LINDETH SILVERDALE

Lindeth Tower, built in 1842 by Henry Paul Fleetwood, a Preston banker who lived at Lindeth Lodge (now Wolf House) and who had an extensive estate in the Lindeth area.

Opposite: The Shieling, built about 1890 for Meta and Julia Gaskell, daughters of Mrs Elizabeth Gaskell. Having enjoyed their childhood visits they came back to live in Silverdale as adults. Subsequently the house was occupied by Gordon Bottomley, the poet, from 1914 to 1948. During his time in Silverdale he amassed a large collection of Pre-Raphaelite paintings. The collection is now on display in Carlisle Museum at Tullie House.

Lindeth Tower is in the grounds of Tower House (datestone 1816). Mrs Gaskell and her two daughters Meta and Julia came here for summer holidays in 1840–60. Mrs Gaskell used the Tower as a place to do her writing.

Above left: Margaret (Meta) Gaskell, d.1913.

Above right: Julia Gaskell, d. 1908.

Gordon Bottomley in his study in the Shieling.

Greywalls. Pearl and Toby Sharp returned to Silverdale in about 1928 and lived in Greywalls (now Ridgeway Park). When Toby died in 1936 his son Edward (affectionately known as Teddy) came to live in Greywalls. Teddy had a passion for gardening.

The front elevation of Greywalls with its fabulous views in the 1930s. Croquet on the lawn appears to have provided something of a distraction from the beauties of the Bay.

Garden Party and Baby Show on front lawn c. 1932. Those present include John Rowland Willan (centre) and Katherine Knight to his left. At the top of the steps is one of the Maclackan boys from Cornerways on Cove Road. It's not known who won the prize for the best baby!!

Teddy Sharp and
his head gardener
Harold Lucas c.1979

Yew Tree House, built by R. J. Bolton in about 1880. The home of Henry Thornton, a widower and retired cab proprietor from Witherslack. He is seen leaning on the rail by the front door.

The side of Yew Tree House, showing Yew Tree Cottage, and with Henry Thornton seated in the grounds.

4

CHURCH AND CHAPEL

BEFORE THE FIRST WORLD WAR, life in the village very much revolved around the church and chapel. Records suggest that there had been a chapel in Silverdale since before the Reformation when it was referred to as a chantry in the Diocese of Worcester. In Pope Gregory's bull in 1233 it was listed as 'Cell at S'dale'. In 1536 Cartmel Priory records talk of a Chapel at Silverdale. It was rebuilt in 1679 and in 1691 the chapel was in the parish of Warton.

The vicar of Warton wanted the good people of Silverdale to attend his services in Warton come hail, rain or shine, rather than having services in their own chapel. One can imagine them tramping along the causeway across Leighton Moss in all shades of weather. There was a protracted legal battle with the Curate of Silverdale vs the Vicar of Warton; the curate's petition indicates that there had been a chapel in Silverdale for about 70 years. The dispute rumbled on from 1686 to 1695. In 1829 the Rev. Carus Wilson of Cove House had the chapel rebuilt with the addition of 207 free seats. The consecration to St John took place when the chapel was reopened in 1829.

Mr Henry Boddington, the Manchester brewer, of Cove House gave the land for, and was a generous benefactor to, the present St John's Church. The Murton family of Highfield contributed generously, and significant sums were also raised by public subscription. Henry Boddington came to live in Silverdale in 1876 and it was his habit to commute to his famous brewery by train. He had a carriage that took him to the station in the morning and collected him on his return. Each day he would travel along Cove Road past the rather lowly Old Chapel. Within three years of his arrival the Methodists had built a fine new church on Cove Road on higher ground than the Old Chapel. In those days there was constant competition for the hearts and minds of the population. The established Church of England saw the growing nonconformist Methodist movement as a threat and it is not difficult to see how the new Methodist church may have rankled with Mr Boddington, a staunch Church of England supporter. It may well have been this that encouraged him to promote the building of a new church, built on ground some 9 metres (30ft) higher than the Methodists', thus restoring the natural order of things!

The old chapel at the junction of Cove Road, Emesgate and Park Road in the early years of the twentieth century after it had been replaced by the new church.

There was limited room for burial plots around the old church so a new cemetery was opened across the road. When the new church was opened the old gravestones from the chapel site were moved to the new church and arranged around the boundary walls (Crosland of Arnside, 1904).

The Methodist Church was built by 1879 at a cost of £1024. In 1896 the school room was added by Christopher Hall the local builder at a cost of £262. The costs were met by generous local benefactors, including Mr Hebden, and through fund raising events. Finally the Hebden family cleared the remaining debts; their generosity is commemorated on a monument adjacent to the church. Today there is a clock over the main window in memory of Willie Riley, the author, who was a tireless worker for Methodism.

Methodism was brought to the area by the Gibsons of Tower Farm. John Hebden of the Woodlands was a member of the Wesleyan Methodist Society and shortly after 1873 he set aside this outbuilding at the Woodlands for meetings and services. Methodism prospered so it was decided that they should build a church, and Mr Hebden offered the site on Cove Road.

WESLEYAN CHURCH, SILVERDALE.

An early photo of the new St John's Church completed in 1886. The shot was taken close to the Post Box now positioned at the entrance to Sarah Fishwick's drive.

It was not until 1883 that work started on the new Parish Church of St John. The land was given by Mr Henry Boddington of Cove House (the Manchester Brewer). The church was designed by Ball & Elce of Manchester and much of the building work was funded by Mr Boddington, together with other local benefactors including Mrs Watson and Mrs Dunn of Hazelwood, and Joseph Walker of The Green, who gave the limestone for the external walls. The Murtons of Highfield on Cove Road also made significant contributions.

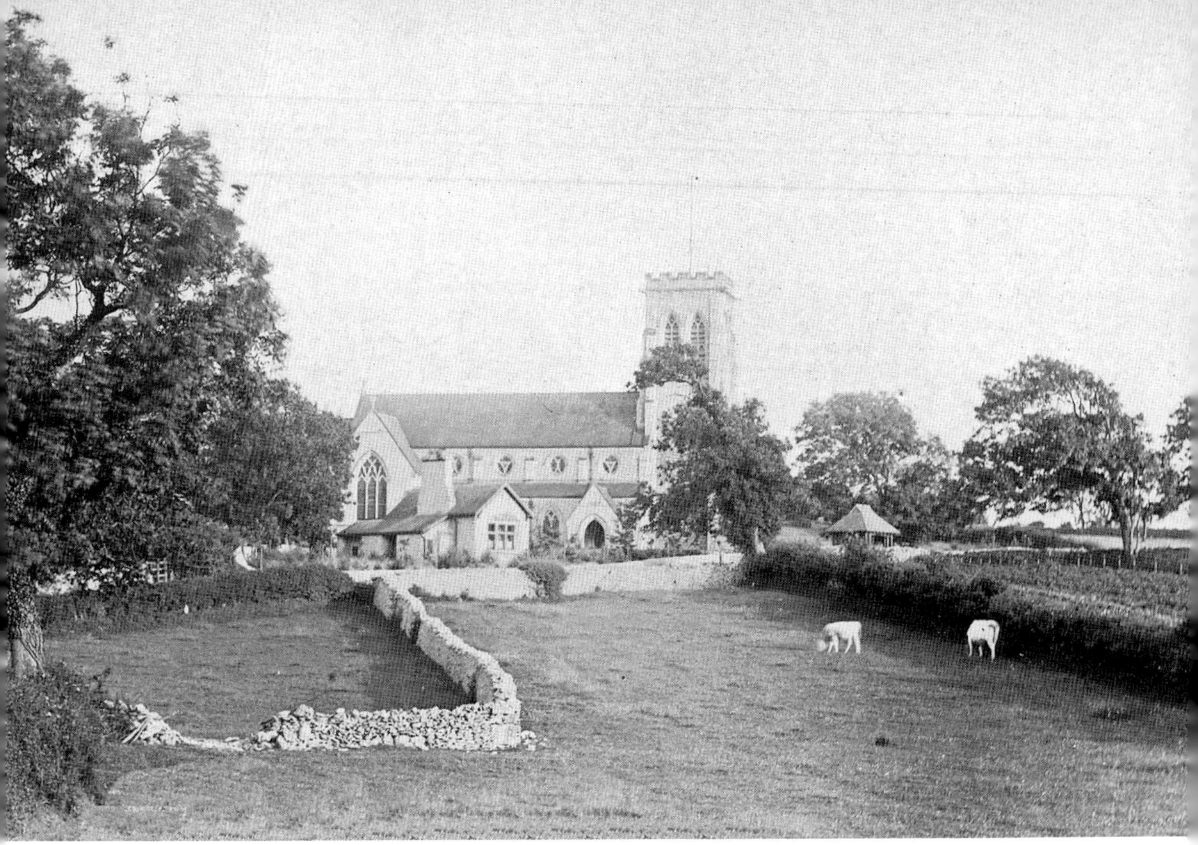

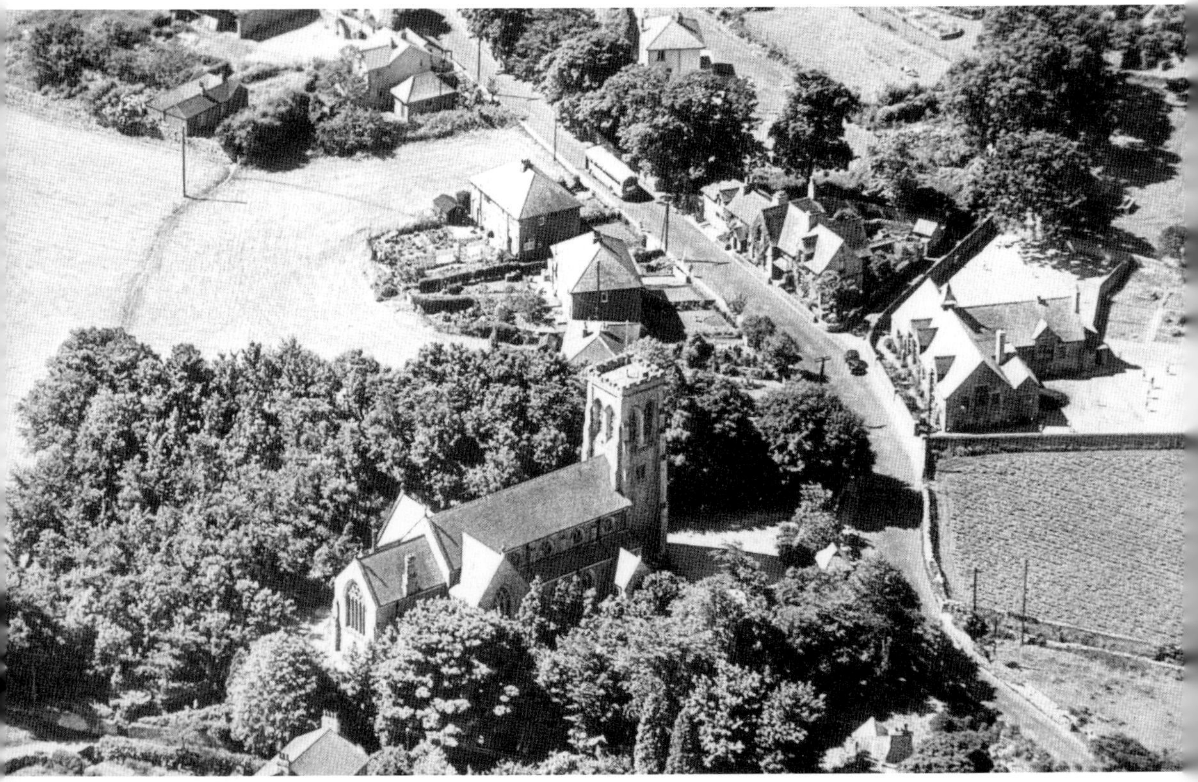

Opposite, top: an early picture of St John's not long after it was opened but before the Church of England school was built opposite the church in 1896. Church Cottage can be seen alongside the church.

Opposite, bottom: a more recent aerial view of St John's Church (in the 1950s) showing the school on the opposite side of Emesgate and the buildings and trees that have grown up around the church.

Church Cottage, built by Henry Boddington in 1886 for Miss Bowles. She was a friend who, like him, suffered from respiratory problems. Pine trees were planted all round the cottage as, at the time, it was thought that the aroma of pine helped with breathing. Here we see Mr Robinson, a later tenant, who added the porch. Many in the village remember more recent tenants, Alberta Johnson and her mother, who opened it as The Wayside Tea Rooms. They sold sweets to school children from the front porch.

This pair of semis, known as Swiss Villas, opposite the church were built by Henry Boddington to accommodate the builders working on the new church. They were then used by the staff from Cove House.

The footpath leading from St John's to Townsfield and Swiss Villas is known as the 'Sufferance Path' and is privately owned. The irony is that it crosses the mediaeval common field known as Townsfield.

This early photo (pre 1897) by Crosland of Arnside was taken before the organ was installed. It is just possible to see part of the window to the right of the altar. This was blocked off when the organ was installed (see below).

Here we see the organ installed to the right of the altar. The organ commemorates Mrs Murton of Highfield and was donated by her brother. The Murton family made numerous gifts, including Shrigley & Hunt stained glass windows, the reredos and carved capitals and corbels. At this time the church was lit by two rows of suspended oil lamps.

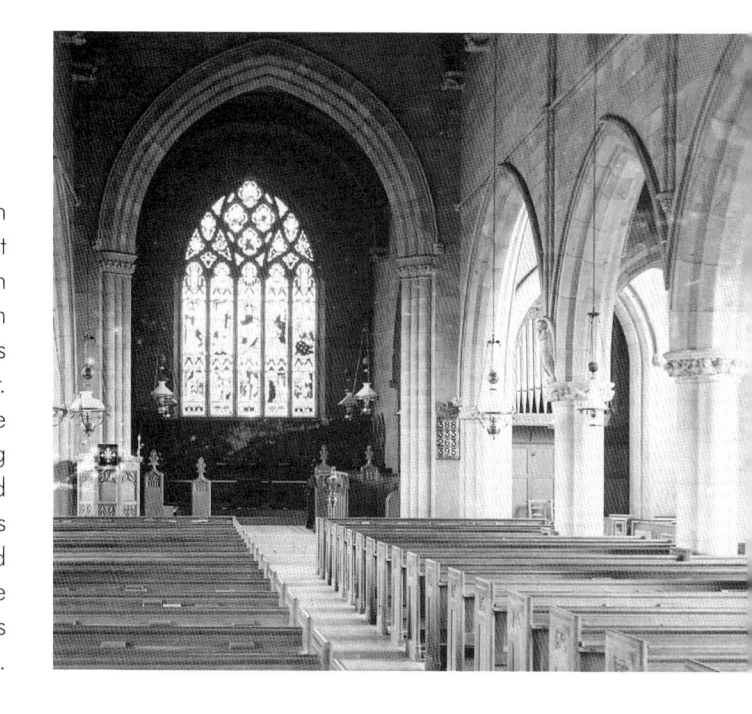

Taken in September 1950 this shows Jackson Taylor the Organist (left), Alberta Johnson the verger, and Robert Christopher Walker the Church Warden (right).

Jackson Taylor was the organist at St John's from 1884 to 1958 when he died, an astonishing 74 years. In his youth he took many pictures used in postcards including the famous card of Townsfield from Cove Road, which includes a young boy standing in the lane. His father, known as 'Honest John Taylor', sold the cards at his grocer's shop in the village. When John died Jackson took over the shop but did not make a success of it. After his first wife died in 1940 he married Enid Parkin, the granddaughter of John Hebden of the Woodlands. Enid was very keen on the history of Silverdale and tried to start a local history society in 1950. They lived in a wooden building on Wallings Lane and when she died in 1955 Jackson deposited her papers and photographs in the County Records Office. Some of the photos in this volume are taken from her collection.

The Parish Church Choir in 1950. On the back row L–R: Barbara Butler, Joan Allinson, Martha Ineson, Jackson Taylor, Enid Parkin, Joan Housley and Joan Taylor. Third row L–R: Betty Bolton and Heather Ineson. Second row L–R: Elsie Alston, Marie Willan, the Rev. Smith, Miss Arnot and Mrs Arnot. Front row L–R: Reg Lucas, Edward Giles, Edward Allinson and Peter Robinson.

Church parade on Stankelt Road shortly after 1900. The brass band is probably the Carnforth Band as, sadly, Silverdale has never had a brass band.

The St John's Church Choir outing to New Brighton in 1950. L–R: Mrs Arnot, Joan Lewis, Elsie Dowthwaite, Isobel Lambert and Joan Arnot.

The St John's Bible Class in 1934 on a fishing and rowing trip to Windermere. L–R: Frank Bolton (Snr), Tom Bolton, Bill Shepherd, Cecil Lockwood, Cecil Hall, Eric Sands, Tommy Dobson, Wilf Bolton and Don Holden. Kneeling is Mr Kellet, the boat hire man at Lakeside.

Silverdale Brownies, possibly on the Institute Field.

The Rev. William Sleigh at the 1939 Jubilee Day celebrations on Woodlands field, here being pushed by Mrs Agnes Walker of Croft Cottage, Stankelt Road. He was the longest serving vicar of Silverdale, holding the post for 45 years. This picture was taken the year after he retired.

This house was built as a vicarage some time after 1807 by Rev. Richard Knagg, curate in charge of the old church. When the new parsonage was built on Cove Road in 1837 this building became known as Walnut Cottage and later Morningside (now No. 51 The Row). The photo was taken in 1908 and shows Mrs Ann Holmes with her daughter Elizabeth Moss and granddaughter Mary.

The new Parsonage on Cove Road was built by Rev. Carus Wilson of Cove House. This followed his rebuilding of the old church in 1829. The Parsonage was completed 1837.

Rev. William Sleigh was very fond of gardening and a great supporter of the Horticultural Society. Here we see him with his prize onions and the Sleigh Cup that he donated to the society and is still presented to winners each year.

Rev. Sleigh, with his carer Agnes Walker seated on his left, on a church outing to Belle Vue in 1937.

St John's Bellringers. L–R: Jack Ambrose, Robert Dowthwaite, Joe Hayton, Walter Howsley Junior, Walter Howsley Senior and one other. Date not known.

St John's Bellringers for Miss Robertshaw's Wedding Day, 16 August 1905. The man in the bowler, Robert Dowthwaite, appears on both this and the previous picture on p. 85.

St John's Sunday School Treat at Bowness in 1929 (smaller children).

St John's Sunday School Treat at Bowness in 1929 (larger boys).

The St John's Church Sunday School Medal given to encourage attendance, particularly during the period between the World Wars.

Hazelwood, built by Leonard Willan in the early 1840s, was a private dwelling for many years for the Willan, Sharp, Dunn and Carrington families. When Mr Carrington of Carrington & Dewhurst died, his widow bequeathed the estate to the Roman Catholic Church. In 1952 a new foundation, St John of God, set up a hospital for the chronically sick. The property had supposedly been in Catholic hands for many years and included a small chapel dedicated to St Gerard, used by the families and neighbouring Catholics.

On 12 June 1952 Hazelwood opened as the St John of God hospital. The opening was carried out by the Bishop of Lancaster, Thomas Flynn. On the right is Brother Brendan Davidson, prior of the new hospital.

A group of brothers at Hazelwood. Rome gave permission to withdraw the religious community from the St John of God Hospital in 1967. In 1968 the Missionary Sisters of Our Lady of the Apostles took over and the place was run as a nursing home till it was sold for redevelopment and converted into apartments.

A group of residents on the south terrace in about 1955. Brother Brendan Davidson, the prior, is standing at the back of the group.

Nativity play in St John's Church 1951, with Christine Letcher as Mary.

5

SCHOOLING IN SILVERDALE

In about 1682 James Atkinson became school master and curate. He held these posts until his death in 1727. He lived and taught at 'Cornerways' at the junction of Cove Road and Emesgate Lane. In 1728 the Burrows' Charity was established by Joseph Burrows of Waterslack. It provided a payment of £2 per annum, conditional upon the curate living in Silverdale and teaching boys and girls to read and write. This reference to the provision of formal education for girls in 1728 must have put Silverdale among the pioneers of women's rights.

A new parsonage was built in 1829. It is not certain where classes were held between then and 1836 when they moved to the building seen on the left in this picture.

Parish Rooms and School. The 1845 OS map shows the rear of the building as the Tithe Barn, however the passing of the Tithe Commutation Act in 1836 left the barn vacant. It was converted to become the school. It was enlarged in 1855 and 1878 but when the new school was built in 1896 it became the Parish Rooms (Village Hall) until 1931. It was converted to dwellings (Old Hall Cottages) in the 1980s.

The laying of the foundation stone for the new school. Henry Boddington's son, Mr W. S. Boddington, was a benefactor to the school. Here he is seen laying the foundation stone in 1896. To the right of Mr Boddington is Christopher Hall, the builder. To his right is the vicar, the Rev. Sleigh. Note St John's Church in the background before it became surrounded by trees.

The new school shortly after completion, much as we see it today. Recent extensions have been added to the left-hand side. When it was first built it had a red tiled roof.

A school group in about 1912 with the schoolmaster Robert Calverley and the mistress Lily Ambrose. Children include Ted Allinson, Tom Lambert and Tommy Hornby on the back row with Wilf Savage in front of the schoolmaster.

May Queen in 1905.

Nursery rhyme costumes in about 1910.

May Queen in 1910.

Schoolmaster Mr Calverley and mistress Miss Waterhouse 1910.

May Queen in 1912. This year's May Queen was Daphne Newman, daughter of the head gardener at Cove House. The schoolmaster Mr Calverley and the staff are standing at the back, and Rev. Sleigh, the vicar, is on the extreme left.

The school senior team of maypole dancers on Woodlands field in 1912.

A good report for a hard working child, Lawrence Richmond, in 1912.

School group in 1937, Mr Winnerah's class. Back row L–R: David Bisbrown, George Thomas, Noel Cannon, Gerald Richardson, Donald Pennington, George Robinson. Third row L–R: Enid Richmond, Elsie Benn, Leslie Swindlehurst, Bessie Hodkinson, Betty Holmes, Margaret Knowles, Edith Walker, Betty Richmond, Fred Fishwick, York Richmond, Emily Robinson. Second row L–R: Ted Winterbottom, Nell Shepherd, Mabel Moorby, Greta Sands, Dorothy Hornby, John Walker. Front row L–R: Fred Cowperthwaite, Ken Hartley, George Mason, Dick Lambert.

1939–40 Miss Gillan's Class. Front row L–R: unknown, Ingram Cowperthwaite, Frank Hartley, Bert Housley, Bob Mason, A. Lambert. Second row: Dorothy Baker, unknown, Phillis Lewis, Joan Lewis, Ruth Holmes, Margaret Dowthwaite, Marie Taylor, Marie Willan, unknown, unknown. Back row: Jackie Woof, unknown, unknown, John Livesey, Cyril Farrar, Rowland Horne, John Rowland Willan. Notice the footwear, which ranges from shoes, boots and wellingtons to clogs!

Opposite: early 1930s class. Back row L–R: Kenneth Walker, Robert Barber, Frank Holmes, Douglas Nicholson, Eddy Glover, Derrick Marsden, John Hodkinson, Ted Holmes, Bill Marsden, Dennis Hamilton, Grenville Keith. Third row L–R: Marjorie Fielding, Beryl Jefferson, Alice Lucas, Jessie Caulton, Gladys Jenner, Kathleen Richmond, Annie Cowperthwaite, Alice Green, Margaret Knowles, Jean Pennington, Mary Taylor, Peggy Tranter. Second row L–R: Jim Hartley, Dora Keith, Dorothy Hornby, Dorothy Rawstron, Vera Hodgson, Bessie Hodkinson, Nellie Shepherd, Betty Richmond, Jim Knowles. Front row L–R: Billy Green, Peter Taylor, Bill Atkinson, George Thomas.

A school class in 1952. Back row L–R: unknown, Ian Metcalf, Laurie McKay, unknown, Trevor Parsons, Tim Proctor. Middle row L–R: Robert Raynor, Robert Shaw, David Raynor, Jeff Casson, David Proctor, Ian McKay, Graham Casson, Robert Bolton. Front row L–R: Doreen Pennington, Jean Edgar, Sue Webber, Doris Taylor, Freda Newton, Margaret Brown, Connie Fishwick, Margaret Dobson, and Vera Clark seated on the floor.

School class in September 1959. Back row L–R: David Lambert, Janet Hodkinson, unknown, Helen Waddington, Bryan McLachlan, unknown, unknown, Angela Richmond, Christopher White, Pauline Robinson. Next to back, standing L–R: Christopher Clark, Stephen Fishwick, Paul Fishwick, Martin Dewhurst, Harry Coleman, David Chapman, Christopher Driver, unknown, Jimmy Mason, Jeffery Nicholls, David Lambert. Seated L–R: Gillian Seddon, Christine Lambert, Marlene Pennington, Alison Pennington, Judith Humphries, Yvonne Nicholls, Barbara Blackwood, Helen Mason, Janet Pennington, Christine Wilkinson. Seated front L–R: Alison Robinson, Angela Holden.

Opposite: a school class in June 1954. Back row L–R: Nigel Lucas, unknown, Robert Shaw, Billy Pennington, Chris Lambert, Alan Hislop, Mick Pennington, Rodney Dolden. Next row, standing: unknown, Tommy Taylor, Tim Proctor, Alan Swindlehurst, Michael Proctor, Malcolm Parsons, Robert Bolton. Next to front row: Jean McKay, Freda Hodgson, Cheryl Richmond, Helen Ringland, Marion Hodkinson, Isobel Smith, Katherine Wells, Angela Bell. Front row: Hazel Quirk, Joan Bennett, Joanna Taylor, unknown, Marie Edgar.

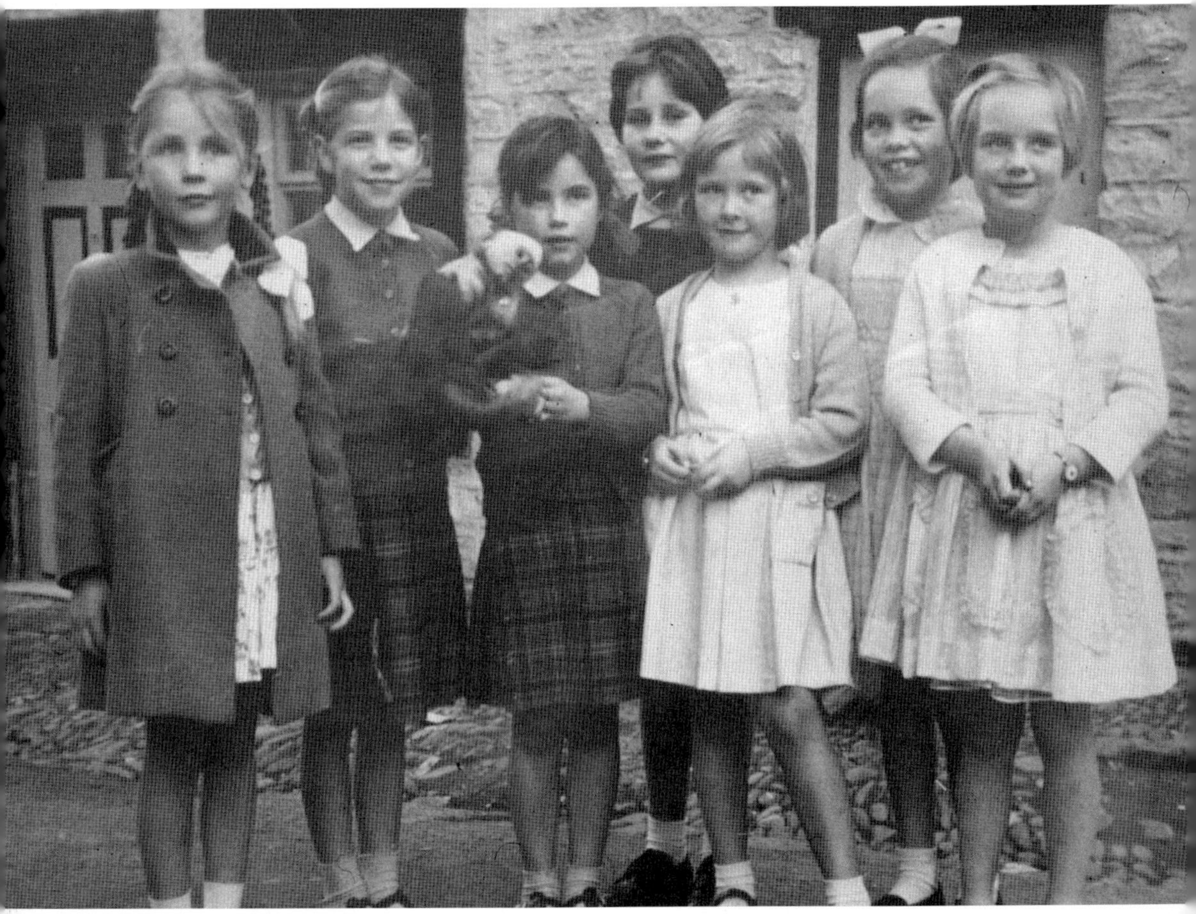

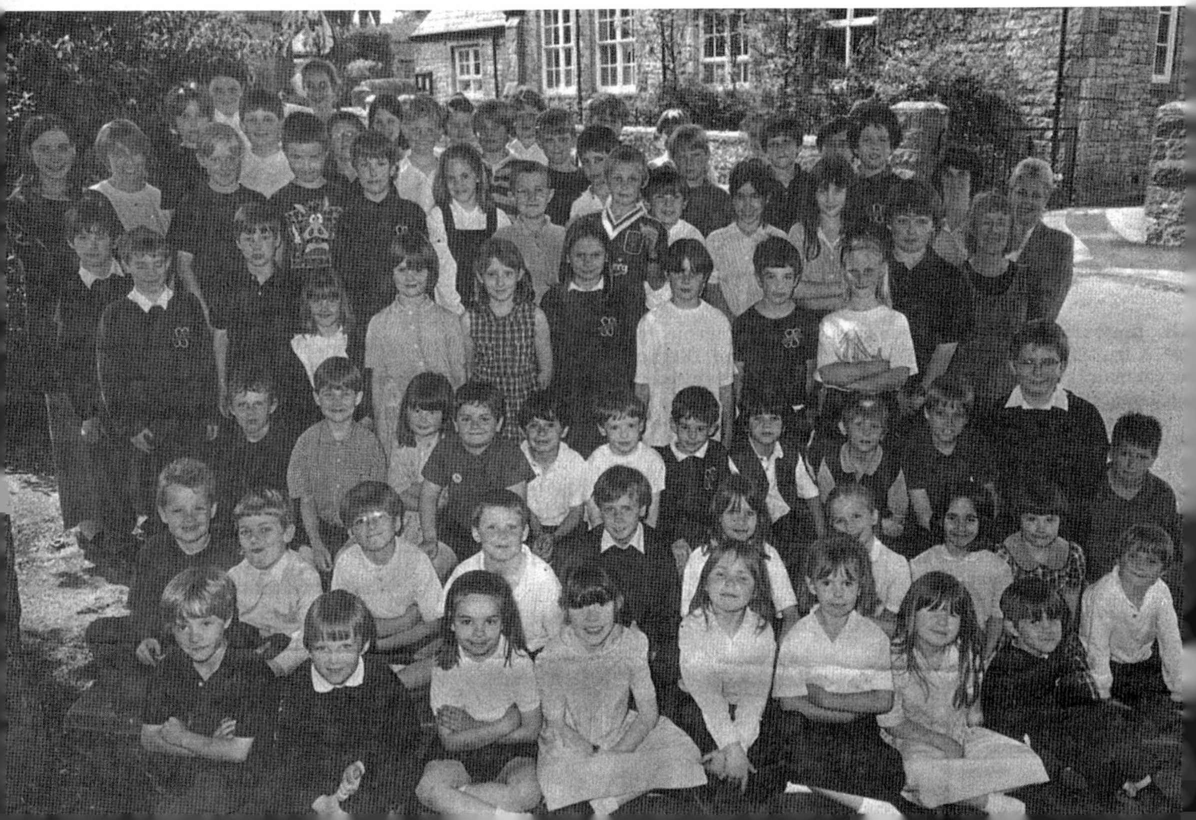

Opposite: schoolgirls in the 1960s. L–R: Dawn Wilkinson, Cheyne and Lyn Martlin, Christine Lambert, Elizabeth Byrom, Janet Hodkinson and Angela Holden.

Staff and students at Bleasdale School in 2000 celebrating the Millennium.

Opposite: a photo celebrating the school centenary in May 1997.

6

THE WORKING DAY

BEFORE THE ARRIVAL OF THE RAILWAY, bringing wealthy incomers and holidaymakers, most locals were employed in three main industries: farming, fishing and quarrying. Of these, farming was probably the most important. For at least two hundred years or more the village consisted of scattered farmsteads and there was no village centre as we know it today. Little changed in the farming community and in farmers' practices until the 1870s when external forces brought the changes described below.

Farming

First let's look at the scattered farms that made up our community and then see some of the farming practices of the period between 1890, when the first photographs were taken, and the time of WWII. Nearly all of the old farmsteads were located around the boundary of the ancient enclosure and those which made up the scattered township of Silverdale are shown in the following photographs.

Bradshaw Gate, Silverdale.

Bottoms Farm (c.1910). The original farm building dates from 1720 but additions were made up to 1900. The present owners, the Lambert family, moved in in 1901 and it is likely that the young man in the garden is one of their sons, either John or Thomas.

Opposite: Bradshaw Gate Farm, 1926. The Bradshaws were corn millers at Bradshaw Gate in the seventeenth century. The Walling family farmed at Bradshaw Gate from 1706 to the 1890s. The ancient enclosure gate was probably located at the right-hand side of the farm where Cove Road is at its narrowest. The last farmers at this farm were the Clarks who left in 1945 when it ceased to be a farm.

Gillian's Farm (before 1910), with a datestone reading 'IB 1780'; John and Isabella Bouskill. Gillian was the wife of Thomas Clark, blacksmith and farmer, who died here in 1717. She survived him by many years and the farm became known as 'Gillian's'. It is thought that a small shop operated from the farm before village shops developed.

Gibraltar Farm. Silverdale.

Row End Farm (1912) at the eastern end of The Row. At this time Joseph Robinson, a retired worsted weaver from Bradford, and his wife were living in the house and it had ceased to be a farm. This picture shows a visit by family and friends.

Green Farm, now known as Crinkle Cottage, was one of the original handful of farms. During later conversion to a dwelling, the dairy on the right became part of the house. For a time the building became known as the 'Oldest House in Silverdale'. A new owner in 1952, having been informed that the house was 500 years old, installed a datestone to that effect over the front door.

Opposite: Gibraltar Farm, probably farmed by the Bennett family when the photo was taken. Michael, his wife Eleanor, their 10 children and a domestic servant, Gertrude Truscot, lived at the farm. Their three eldest sons (14–16 years) were already working on the farm. It is Mrs Eleanor Bennett here working as dairy maid. Recording of female farm workers in Census records was very hit and miss and it is not possible to be sure of women's roles on the farms of the area.

Waithman's House Farm on Lindeth Road. Datestone over door 'William Waithman & Dorothy his wife 1739'. Parts of the house are thought to be earlier. Waithman was a Quaker and ran a farmers' bank from this house. For many years this has been the home of the family of Reginald Kaye, Silverdale's celebrated plantsman.

Bank House Farm included a house, a cottage and threshing barns. A firehouse and parlour were added in the late 1600s. The later additions included a 'Lantern Window'. It was bought by the Bisbrown family in 1597 who farmed here for nearly 300 years. The farm with 57 acres was donated to the National Trust in 1983 by Tom Bright of Cove House. Today the National Trust has a local office in the outbuildings.

Red Bridge Farm, home of the Edmondsons who also ran a local carting or haulage business. The man in the distance appears to be collecting horse manure from the road. This was a valuable fertiliser a hundred years ago.

Waterslack Farm. There was a horse gin that used to drive a threshing machine at the back of the barn. For many years it was the home of the Walker family. The 1909 valuation described it as a 'nice farm' but rainwater was the only source of drinking water.

Slackwood Farm. This picture was taken in the early 1950s when the Fishwick family were the tenants. They were at the farm from before WWII till 1976. The blocked bedroom windows may date from the 'window tax' days, the act itself not repealed until 1851.

In the 1870s Silverdale suffered a series of very wet summers when crops did not ripen and at times were unharvestable. This was accompanied by the start of cheap grain imports from the USA. Combined, these had two impacts on Silverdale farming. Firstly, many farms were sold, and secondly, farming practices changed and grazing for dairy cows and cattle rearing increased as cereal production was not able to compete with cheap imports. New owners and tenants moved towards more modern farming practices but some cereal production continued up to WWII. In addition, land was marketed as desirable building land; piecemeal sales went on steadily, reaching a peak in the 1960–70s with the development of bungalow estates within the ancient enclosure land.

Livestock consisted of milk and beef cattle, sheep, pigs and hens; horses were bred as working animals. Crops were oats, barley and wheat alongside root crops of potatoes, turnips, carrots, mangold-wurzels and swedes. The photographs and postcards that follow were selected in an attempt to cover as many of the farming activities as space would permit.

For many years the Longhorn breed was preferred in northern Lancashire, but during the 1800s the Shorthorn was introduced. The Shorthorn was favoured for its greater milk yield at a time when demands for fresh milk were increasing in the cities, and the rail and road links were providing a speedy delivery system to serve these expanding markets.

From 1900 onwards, local farmers began to introduce other breeds to improve milk yields and meat production. Friesians, Holsteins, Ayrshires and Jerseys, for example, became more popular and helped with the development of new local milking herds and beef cattle.

Grazing Shorthorns in the fields in front of The Row (photo: Lilyland Series by D.J. Wilson of Arnside Post Office, about 1910).

William Walker of Waterslack Farm with a young Friesian bull (1935).

Cattle watering at Bank Well on The Row in 1908 before houses, trees and undergrowth changed the appearance of the area. The cowherd was Mr Rawlinson, a local farmer (photo by Grayston Bird of Bath, a visiting photographer).

Masham sheep grazing on the salt marsh near the Cove (Crosland of Arnside, pre 1911). Note the castellated wall of Cove House and The Oratory on the cliff top in the distance.

Blue faced Leicesters grazing on salt marsh (photo: Grayston Bird, 1908). Thousands of sheep and lambs grazed on the shore and were only taken off during very high tides.

Sheep washing near the Cove (photo: Crosland of Arnside, pre 1911). The farmer in the straw hat throwing in the sheep is Mr Clark of Bradshawgate Farm and the man next him is Mr John Walker, the owner of the horse and cart. Earlier there had been a sheep breed known as the 'Silverdale' but by 1900 it had been largely replaced by the Masham breed seen here.

At times the sheep on the marsh wandered into the channels and got bogged down in the quicksand. Here we see one being rescued and it appears that in these emergencies it was a case of all hands to the pump. The man holding the head is Mr Newman of Cove Cottage, the head gardener at Cove House (c.1910).

A small flock of sheep being driven up Emesgate Lane. Sheep movement must have been a common sight in the village when the lanes were largely clear of motor vehicles. The photo was taken just below St John's Church but with a clear view of the Methodist Church prior to the building of bungalows and houses.

William Walker of Waterslack Farm shearing his sheep, ably assisted by his son, the late John Walker of Lakeside View.

Shearing by the farmer Fredrick Bethell at Bankhouse Farm, watched by his children Richard, Walter and Katherine, in June 1910.

Farmer John Hodgson feeding the pigs at Bradshawgate Farm, watched by Henry Thornton of Yew Tree House and accompanied by his granddaughter Phyllis May Snowden.

Feeding the hens at Bradshawgate Farm.

Fred Burrow and his nephew ploughing Levens Field.

Henry Thornton of Yew Tree House with the stallion and groom, John Hodgson Jnr of Bradshawgate Farm. Mr Thornton was a retired 'Cab Proprietor' and clearly maintained a keen interest in horses.

The Burrows family bred heavy horses at Myers Farm (now owned by the RSPB). The horses were used to pull the carts of the coal business that was also run from the farm.

Jack Holmes with the Waterslack horses Tommy, Duke and Jammie in a carnival procession about 1912.

This 1907 photo of Cove Road by Hawthorn Bank perhaps demonstrates the pace of life in the village in the early 1900s. It was fine to let your horse graze on the grass of the verge. An obstruction like this would cause traffic tailbacks in both directions in less than a minute today!

Silverdale Loyalty, one of Mr Bright's polo ponies bred in the village on the fields that now make up The Lots. Mr Mason of Bankhouse Farm was the groom. Herbert Bright, cousin to John Bright the reformer, lived at Cove House (1920–50) and had a very successful polo pony stud for many years.

Three-horse heavy haulage rig on Park Road, Pye's cottages just visible behind the cart. The young man standing by the horses is Dick Moss, whose name now appears on the village war memorial amongst those killed in WWI.

Richard and John Edmondson of Red Bridge Farm carrying turves from Hawes Water or Silverdale Moss in about 1910.

Fred Burrow ploughing on Townsfield (about 1950).

Jack Lambert ploughing in the ancient enclosure to the east of Bottoms Lane.

Root crops growing in Townsfield. The Queen Victoria Jubilee Monument (The Pepper Pot) stands clear on a rather bare Castlebarrow largely devoid of trees. At this time Castlebarrow was grazed by sheep, which kept tree growth to a minimum.

Harvesting a cereal crop in the ancient enclosure land by Bottoms Lane. On the machine is John Jackson Lambert accompanied by one of the young Lambert boys. The spectators include Mr Newman, Cove House head gardener, whom we saw earlier helping to dig out a sheep stuck in the quicksand. Note the stooks built with sheaves to dry the corn.

A horse-drawn binder operated by the Robinson family from Tower Farm.

Corn stooks in Clark's field, beside Emesgate Lane.

All the crop safely gathered in – Mr Clark of Bradshawgate Farm and his colleague John Walker have time to take the local children on a joy ride on Townsfield. John Walker was also the local night soil collector.

Celebration at Waterslack Farm with a special meal laid on by Mrs Walker for all those who helped with the threshing (1930). Clockwise from the door: Tamar Walker, William Walker Snr, Jackie Woof, unknown, Doug Fishwick, Raymond Holmes, Syd Meadows, Gerald Richardson, Robert Barber, John Swindlehurst, unknown, unknown, unknown, Betty Williams, unknown, unknown.

William Walker lifting potatoes in Letterbox Lot at the end of Park Road.

Ploughing the field between Elmslack and Cove Road on 13 May 1952. The field was then planted with mangolds, turnips, peas, cabbages, carrots and kale. A real mixed crop!

Clem Proctor and son of Know Hill Farm, haymaking in the field below the Silverdale Hotel on Shore Road. On the right-hand side can be seen the corner of the hotel swimming pool.

Haymaking on what is now the Silverdale Children's Playing Field. The photograph was taken from Elmslack looking towards the village and shows how little house building had taken place by 1910.

William Walker returning to Waterslack Farm with a full cart of hay, watched by his daughter Tamar (left).

Fishing

For many centuries Morecambe Bay has yielded a bountiful harvest of seafood. The main catches from Silverdale included flukes, cockles and prawns, with much of the fishing carried out using horse and cart. At low tide, when vast tracts of sand – extending up to 8 miles out – were exposed, boats were of little use. So working out on the sands required an intimate knowledge of the ever-changing sandbanks and channels. The work was arduous and continued in wind, rain, cold and even fog. Tide cycles, not the clock, dictated the working day and it was not uncommon to see carts leaving and returning in the dark. The cockling beds were four or five miles out and occasionally fishermen were lost, overtaken by the incoming tide.

Cockles were, by far, the most profitable catch on the Silverdale side of the bay. From the village it was rarely less than a couple of hours' journey out to the cockling beds, crossing marshland, wet sand and mud, and, of course, there were channels to be crossed before reaching the beds.

Cockles were gathered using a 'craam', a three-pronged hand fork on a foot-long handle. The work was laborious and back breaking, involving being bent double and scooping up enough cockles to fill a sack. A sack was the minimum amount required to make 'wages'. Cockles were scooped into the baskets seen in the back of the cart in the picture below, and each sack held about two and a half baskets. The cockles were brought up to the surface of the sand either by stamping on the sand in a circular fashion or using a 'jumbo'. This consisted of a large flat board up to five feet long with two handle bars. The board was rocked and bounced on the sand to bring the cockles to the surface.

Bob and Lizzie Wilson of Bolton-le-Sands, off to the cockling beds, baskets at the ready.

A group of Silverdale cocklers (c.1910) using 'jumbos' to bring the cockles to the surface where they are being harvested with 'craams' into woven baskets. The work is being carried out by husband and wife partnerships, however the wife's contribution was rarely, if ever, recognised in the census of that time.

The couple, William Burrow and his wife, were on the sands in 1905 (Wilson of Arnside) and Lizzie Wilson in the picture on the right is pictured in 1955 (Hardman of Kendal) holding a 'craam', showing that little had changed other than the introduction of more durable waterproof clothing.

Fred Burrows, father of Nick, out on the sands in the 1960s, when tractor and trailer had taken over from the horse and cart. Here Fred and his colleague are having a well-earned break after a hard day on the sands, judging by the number of sacks of cockles on the trailer.

The cockles were still collected with jumbo, woven basket and a craam, but with a longer handle. The sacks were stacked and kept wet on the shore till they were taken to the station and loaded on a special wagon behind passenger trains heading for the cities to the south.

Tom Webster of No.3 Fisherman's Cottages is returning home after setting his 'Stake Nets' to catch flukes. These fascinating flat fish come in with the tide to feed on the shellfish. The net bottoms opened landward but closed against the stakes as the tide retreated, thus trapping the flukes. The fishermen had to be at the nets as the tide went out otherwise the gulls got the fish. Fluke were also caught with horse-drawn dragnets in the channels.

Shore or Fisherman's Cottages in 1906 (Crosland of Arnside) with the stake nets hung on the wall to be dried, cleaned and mended. Tom Webster lived at the third door from the right. Flukes were also caught from boats by line.

These sail boats were prawners, the design being known as the Lancashire Nobby, and many of the boats in this 1905 photograph were made at the Crosfields boatyard in Arnside. Boats large and small were used for fishing, however during the summers the fishermen supplemented their income by offering pleasure trips for the tourists.

Waterslack Cottage 1939–45, with Mrs Lydia Hartley and son Bill selling flukes to a buyer from Bolton.

Opposite: John Hall, a local fisherman, is seen standing in his boat named Unity. Sadly the Unity was smashed in the gales of 1907. After this disaster Mr Hall, of Rose Cottage, Bottoms Lane, does not appear to have returned to fishing but turned to the land for the rest of his working life.

Joyrides along the shore! Hilda Letcher and friend being given a ride in the shandry cart by her brothers Tom and George Webster in about 1935.

Quarrying

Limestone quarrying has taken place for many years in the Silverdale area. Early work provided building and walling stone together with lime produced by burning the stone in local kilns. Lime was used for improving land and was the prime ingredient in the production of lime mortars and whitewash. It was the coming of the railway in 1857 that led to a major expansion of quarrying activity, particularly at Trowbarrow. Rail sidings were built at Trowbarrow Lime Works, which enabled quarry products to be transported far and wide.

The business expanded with the construction of the Hoffman Kiln, which allowed continuous lime burning. In the 1880s and 1890s there were just over a dozen local men working at Trowbarrow. During this period the owner was James Ward and it was he who developed the process for the production of tar macadam. He marketed his new invention as 'Quarrite', the dustless paving. By 1898 the first 'paving plant' was erected and by 1906 the plant had been expanded. Ward founded Northern Quarries Ltd and by 1900 he was employing over 40 local men in the quarry and the lime and paving (tarmac) works. Quarrite was the first tarmac to be used in the UK, in about 1904. The Northern Quarries Ltd were taken over by Tarmac Ltd. After WWII some 50% of production of limestone went to Dorman Long Steel Company at Middlesborough to be used as flux in steel making. At this stage most of the building stone, tarmac and lime left the site in lorries. The quarry closed in 1965 and the plant was demolished the following year.

A group of 'Limestone Quarrymen', as they were called in the 1911 census, seen at Trowbarrow Quarry about 1910. There has been a suggestion that this may not be Trowbarrow but at least three of these men appear on a photo of the crushing plant at the limeworks and other village pictures.

This probably dates from about 1910. The quarry is seen on the right of the skyline. From the quarry the stone was taken to the limeworks on a wagon track following the line of bushes along the field boundary. This was later improved with the installation of a chain-operated incline using a gravity system.

Opposite: Trowbarrow Quarry during its later operational days, the tramway can be seen heading towards the northern end of the quarry. The large block had, for many years, provided shelter for shot firers and the workforce during blasting. The photo was taken in the early 1960s before its final closure by Tarmac in 1965.

TROWBARROW WORKS, SILVERDALE.

Here we see the crusher and the tar macadam plant on the right, together with the company's wagons waiting to be loaded on the sidings alongside the Furness Railway main line. On the centre left is the Hoffman Kiln, designed to produce a continuous supply of lime by burning a stone and coke mix within the oval tunnel kiln.

The tars used to coat the limestone chippings to make tarmac were highly flammable and in January 1908 there was a disastrous fire which destroyed most of the plant.

FIRE AT TROWBARROW LIME WORKS, JAN. 30. 08. (2)

All that was left of the 'Quarrite' or tarmac plant after the fire in 1908. The covered wagons on the siding in front of the plant were used to transport lime in the dry. It is just about possible to see the name on the wagons, it reads 'Northern Quarries Co. Ltd. Trowbarrow Lime Works Silverdale No. 33 Furness Railway'.

A group of men from the limeworks. The photograph is taken outside one of the entrances to the Hoffman Kiln.

Quarrymen outside loco shed in August 1926. Back row L–R: Laddie Taylor, unknown, Joe Bennett, Dick Hewitson, Bill Simpson, Tom Battersby. Front row L–R: Stan Walker, unknown, Walter Dobson, George Proctor, Harold Braithwaite, Syd Walker.

Tarmac road surfacing comes to Silverdale in 1936. The machine belongs to All Weather Gravelling Co. of Victoria Street London. Len Humberstone and his co-driver Bill Pigson were engaged by the local council.

Many of the quarry workers lived in the houses in Northern Terrace on the road to Haweswater but close to the quarry. In the 1911 census every house was occupied by quarry workers and their families.

A street party for the Northern Terrace families to celebrate VE day. Those present include the Penningtons, Pearsons, Hileys, Crisps, Hudson, Edgars, Swindlehurst, Wincap and Woofs. A goodly collection of village family names.

Land Reclamation

In the early 1870s, Herbert J. Walduck of West Lindeth, mining owner and agent, set about obtaining parliamentary powers to reclaim the bay for agricultural use. His first submission involved a scheme to enclose the whole area between Park Point, Arnside, to Hest Bank (over 6000 acres). Local objections were raised as the people of Silverdale had been given rights to graze and fish on the shore in the Enclosure Act Award (1811–17). After consideration by parliamentary committee the Act was finally passed to allow the area between Jenny Brown's Point and Hest Bank to be reclaimed. Walduck had started even before the Act was passed. He opened a quarry at Jenny Brown's and proceeded to construct an embankment out into the bay.

A railway was constructed to get the stone from the quarry to the embankment and the road to Jenny Brown's was carried over the track on a bridge, as shown on this pencil sketch opposite by Phil Marriner, sold as a postcard.

Mr Walduck appointed Captain Mutter, a retired sea captain from Whitby, to supervise the work and things moved on apace. A steam loco was acquired to draw the stone wagons instead of horses. The intention was to construct an embankment straight out into the bay for just over a mile. Unfortunately the consulting engineers underestimated the amount of stone required to make a stable level structure on the shifting sands of Morecambe Bay. The extra cost meant that funds from the original stock issue were running out, so attempts were made to issue additional stock. Investors did not have the appetite for it, however. Despite strenuous efforts, Walduck failed to raise sufficient funds.

In 1879 Captain Mutter was crushed when a horse pulling a full stone wagon bolted, de-railed the wagon and spilled its load on him. He died within four days. After this the work on the embankment slowed. Lack of funds, and setbacks in his mining ventures and Carnforth Ironworks all conspired to frustrate Walduck, the energetic entrepreneur. Disaster struck in 1891 when his wife died. Walduck died 8 months later whilst on a visit to Windsor. This brought all work on the reclamation scheme to an end.

The reclamation scheme brought work to the area for over fifteen years. Above is the last man to work on the scheme, John Allinson of The Grove (Refreshments Room) on Shore Road.

At times the embankment is still visible, however it has now been breached in places and is occasionally covered by the bay's shifting sands.

7

LIFE IN THE VILLAGE

Ann Holmes (80 years old), her daughter Elizabeth Moss (35 years old) and granddaughter Mary A. Moss (7 years old) at Walnut Cottage, no. 51 The Row in 1907. Ann was a widow but made a living as a laundress with her daughter. Ann is wearing clothes typical of the older working women over 100 years ago. Caps, shawls and wraparound pinafores were the order of the day.

'Auld Willy' Hall (75 years old), a retired gardener, taking his ease outside Gibraltar Cottage in 1911. Working clothes included rounded raised peak caps, collarless shirts, waistcoats jackets and trousers of coarse worsted or mole skin. Clogs were the working footwear of the time, quite often combined with shin guards. On this occasion 'Auld Willy' appears to have no intention of working!

Frances Parkin's house on the corner of Townsfield on a wonderfully peaceful Cove Road. Next door to her house was the village police station. The sign can just be seen above the door under the bedroom window sill. Police Constable William Halford was resident here at the time and the house had a lockup in the cellar.

Opposite: in the rose garden which preceded the bowling club on Cove Road we see Frances Parkin and her daughter Enid quite elegantly attired and taking tea outside the summer house. Frances was the daughter of John Hebden of the Woodlands. She lived in the end house before Townsfield and described herself as a widow of independent means.

Agnes Walker of Croft Cottage (now Pointer House) entertaining the children on the shore. They all appear to be wearing their 'Sunday Best'. Agnes took on many roles in the village, these included acting as a companion to the elderly and infirm, caring for the sick and laying out the dead. It seems likely that she also acted as midwife.

Jessie Holmes, wife of Robert, with their children Mary, Frank and Thomas William outside their house, Greystones, on The Green in 1910.

Billy Rawlinson, Fred Clarke and Jack Dobson dressed for some special occasion. Fred Clarke was the Silverdale Sub-Postmaster; Billy and Jack worked for Northern Quarries. It is a tradition in the village that young men are given nicknames; some are given alternative first names and others are burdened with less than flattering names. The practice continues to this day amongst some of the long-established village families.

The Silverdale Stag Hunt assembling at the far end of Park Road before WWI. The hunt does not appear to be well supported, for there are many spectators and few riders. The hunt seems to have been short lived and its history has been lost in the mists of time.

Golf Links, Silverdale

Silverdale's nine hole golf course, opposite the village railway station. There are many spectators but only one golfer in this shot, bending to address the ball on a grassy knoll a little to the right of centre. He seems to have a caddie standing to the left of him below the crest of the mound.

Silverdale Rovers Football Club in the 1924–25 season. This was obviously the junior team, when compared with the team described as Silverdale FC that is shown on the next photograph. Back row L–R: Mr Cornthwaite, Jimmy Cornthwaite, George Nicholson, A. Cornthwaite, Harry Burrow, Rivers Lockwood, Jack Taylor, Walter Housley, unknown. Front row: unknown, Tom Savage, Rowland Horn, Vic Hornby and Ted Allinson.

Back row L–R: Harry Hodgson, Stan Walker, Harvey Burrow, David Lee, Jonathon Holden, Joe Bisbrown, George Walker. Centre row: Oliver Holden, George Riding, unknown. Front row: Jimmy Smith, Victor Burrow, Stan Burrow, Harry Ineson and George Tyson.

The Football Club tea ladies in the 1950s. L–R: Mrs Burrow, Freda Hodgson, Martha Ineson, Brenda Farrer, Hilda Letcher and Florence Dyson.

Silverdale FC in 1935. Back row L–R: Bill Green, Bobby Barber, Derek Marsden, Frank Holmes, Doug Nicholson, A. Richmond. Front row: George Mason, Bill Atkinson, Jimmy Knowles, A. Taylor and Jim Hartley.

The Cricket Team in 1939. Back row L–R: Bert Mason, Bill Baines, Ken Hewitson, Harold Hisom, Tommy Dobson, Jack Tallow. Centre row: Harry Ineson, Fred Hisom, Jack Lane, Don Holden. Front row: Gilbert Lambert, Bart Lucas and Bill Shepherd.

A group of members of the Silverdale Tennis Club pause for a photo by the court. It was located on the flat ground between Clarence Farm and Hazelwood.

A quiet afternoon on the bowling green in the 1950s. Attire back then seems far more formal than in more recent times.

An afternoon stroll to the Buck Stone across the road from Challen Hall. This photo was taken in the early 1900s, and today the view looks quite different as a large barn has been built behind the stone. Folklore has it that a large serpent came out of Hawes Water, wrapped itself round the base of the rock and lay hidden until lunch came strolling by.

Lazy days of summer! Reggie and Marion Kaye, founders of the famous Kayes Nursery on Lindeth Road. They are in the company of Frances Wilkinson, wife of Major Wilkinson of Hatchstead on The Row.

A stroll through the village with time to stop for a chat (Matthews Bradford, 1925). The car is parked outside the building which became Silverdale Library in about 1965. Across the road next to Dowthwaite's tearooms was a second café run by the Huthersall family. The sign is high on the end wall to the right of the telegraph pole.

On the left is John 'Coggie' Hall, brother of 'Auld Willy' Hall, dressed in his working garb. He had been a fisherman and cockler but his boat Unity was smashed in the gales of 1907. On the right is Wyn Glover in a post office uniform. Wyn delivered the mail during WWII, standing in for her husband Eddy when he was called up to the RAF.

The village postman Thomas Glover with his wife and son Eddy outside their cottage on Moss Lane in the 1920s.

Grandma and Grandad Clarke with Ivy (later Mrs Taylor) taking a moment on their bench outside Bradshawgate Farm in the 1930s. Teas and refreshments were on sale at the farm. Grandad Clark is seen earlier in the farming section, washing sheep on the shore and giving joy rides to the local children on Townsfield.

The Gaskell Memorial Hall, Silverdale.

After much fund raising far and wide, work began on the Gaskell Memorial Hall which was to replace the Parish Rooms. It was opened in 1931 by Mrs Bright of Cove House. The Silverdale Village Players (SVP) thrived in the 1920s but space was at a premium in the Parish Rooms and many aspects of the new hall were designed specifically to accommodate the SVP. In the early days, lighting and electricity were provided by the Bleasdale House generator next door.

The SVP production 'Painted Sparrows' in March 1938. Standing L–R: Ted Martindale, Len Clark, Lance Hodgson, Mary Richardson, Douglas Nicholson and Fred Allinson. Seated L–R: Lottie Clark, Edith Winterbottom and Mabel Pennel.

The SVP 1948 production 'Ladies in Retirement' starring Edna Marriner, Molly Lockwood, Ellen Richmond, David Bisbrown, Mattie Walker, Hilda Letcher and Joan Calverley.

An SVP production in the 1970s, 'Who Lies There.' Standing L–R: Fred Booth, Margaret Lambert, Eddy Willan, Robert Bolton, Simon Waterhouse, Mavis Bolton. Seated L–R: Mabel Booth, Helen Waddington and Pat Simpson.

Beauty competitions were held in the Gaskell Hall in the 1960s. On the left is Jean Letcher and next but one is Ann Veevers with her sister Jill on the extreme right.

The Silverdale Variety Group entertained the residents of Stonebower and St John of God with The Black and White Minstrels Show in the 1960s. The director was Mr Booth, who is standing at the back on the right.

The Silverdale Variety Group put on fundraising shows and used the money to buy Christmas presents for the residents of Stonebower and St John of God.

'Hawaiian Girls' tableau with Ellen Byron, Bessie Webber, Joan Quirk and Hilda Letcher in the Gaskell Hall. The show was put on to entertain the WI Christmas Party

Below: the Women's Institute New Year party held in the Gaskell Hall 1978. Mabel Pennel is cutting the cake.

Silverdale firemen out on practice in 1958. L–R: Maurice Bainbridge, Bernard Farrer, Chappie Shaw, Harry Dyson and Wilf Bolton.

Although Silverdale has not been blessed with a brass band we did for a time have 'Tom Bolton's Oakland Orchestra', a dance band made up almost entirely of members of the Bolton family.

The Silverdale Handbell Ringers giving a concert in the Gaskell Hall in 1953. Back row L–R: Robert Holmes, Sam Letcher, Frank Bolton Jnr, Cedric Dyson, Cecil Lockwood Jnr, Charlie Webber. Front row L–R: Harry Dyson, Roger Wood, Frank Bolton Snr, Frank Holmes, Wilf Bolton, Cecil Lockwood Snr, and Jim Bolton. All were under the baton of Tom Bolton, the conductor.

Silverdale Girl Guides Camp at Hawkshead in May 1948. Back row L–R: Dorothy Brown, Dorothy Baker, Marie Willan, Mrs Willan, Mrs Arnott, Ruth Arnott, Bessie Bolton, Wilf Bolton, Mrs Marshall, unknown. Front row L–R: unknown x 3, Joan Housley, Margaret Brown, Monica Farrer, Barbara Butler, Margaret Shaw, Jaqui Bolton, Ann Meeks and Robert Meeks.

Left: Wilf Bolton selling ices at the Shore Café and holding a very young Jim Bolton aloft. *Right*: Washington Edgar, said to be the oldest paperboy in Silverdale.

Joan Quirk and young Hazel out in the snow in January 1958.

Silverdale School Nativity play in 1951, the children posing in their costumes for the photo in the school yard.

Gardner's Stores on Stankelt Road (1960s). Fresh pies and sausages were delivered on a Wednesday afternoon. Word soon got around and the queue would quickly develop.

Leeds Poor Children's Holiday Camp, Silverdale 3612

Although the Leeds Children's Holiday Centre (LCHC), formerly known as Leeds Poor Children's Holiday Camp, is just over the border in Cumbria, it has always been regarded as part of the village.

The LCHC was opened in 1905 by the mayor of Leeds and has been in operation for the last 110 years. The village has taken the camp to its heart and has provided much-needed support.

Opening Ceremony, June 8 1905, Leeds Poor Children's Summer Camp

The LCHC offices in Leeds with children waiting to go on their adventure to the seaside.

This photo was taken in 1905 and was used with several others on the original fundraising campaign. It was displayed under the title 'From the Slums' and shows this group of young 'urchins' outside the Leeds LCHC office.

The mêlée at Leeds railway station where obviously anxious mothers are packing their offspring onto the train and into the unknown.

Beds in one of the dormitories at LCHC (photo Matthews, c.1920) By today's standards the beds look rather packed in and the dorm lacking in modern amenities. It is perhaps worth remembering though that this might have seemed like paradise to the children, as many of them would have grown up sharing beds with none-too-clean linen.

This rather damaged shot of the dining room suggests that children were well fed. Again, regular meals and good food were likely to be new experiences for many of the children.

Fresh air, exercise and an introduction to the countryside were all part of the stay. In addition they were all given swimming lessons in the LCHC new pool.

Clearly the visit to Silverdale LCHC had the desired effect, judging by the smiles on the faces of these boys on the train back to Leeds. What started in 1905 continued until 2016, when the last children left on 2 September and the centre closed due to lack of funding. Sad to say, no more children will benefit from a brief stay in Silverdale at the Leeds Children's Holiday Centre.

The LCHC was funded by Leeds City Council but this was supplemented by regular donations from the Royal Navy Ark Royal and by local fundraising in Silverdale. The Rev. Colman and Willy Riley, the author, were part of the local committee, along with Mr and Mrs Farrer, the centre managers, seen on the right.

Across the road from the LCHC and again in Cumbria, despite the address on this postcard, is Holgate's Caravan Park. What started as a small low-key activity has now grown to the point where Silverdale's population almost doubles in the summer time.

The dispersed pitches for touring vans in the 1950s.

Gradually the site grew, with increasing numbers of static caravans and touring pitches, until it reached its present size.

Along with the increasing numbers of vans came the development of visitor facilities. The features shown here have, in recent times, been further enhanced with the provision of an indoor pool and many other state-of-the-art facilities, all helping to make the visitors' 'Silverdale Experience' even more enjoyable.

SILVERDALE

The village celebrates the Coronation of King George V in 1911. The photograph shows a parade on Emesgate, near the Royal. Local dignitaries include Major Morley Saunders of Cove House and Mr Pratt of the Woodlands. Both are attired in morning suits; Mr Pratt is the shorter of the two with a face wreathed in white whiskers. The Carnforth Brass Band is present to help proceedings along.

This enormous bonfire or beacon was lit on Castlebarrow to proclaim the coronation of King George V and Queen Mary on 22 June 1911.

8

DARK DAYS OF WAR

Sergeants Hall and Ion of Silverdale with the 'Territorials' of the Kings Own Royal Lancashire Regiment on summer camp at Hornby in 1911. Many of these men became the backbone of the British Army when war broke out in 1914.

Lancashire Defence Volunteer Brigade, Silverdale Detachment WWI (1918) under the command of Lt John Hutton on the left. Back row L–R: Bobby Holmes, J. R. Bolton, G. Nicholson, W. Housley, S. Walker, Harry Hodgson, Edwin Hall, Joe Hisom. Front row L–R: Townson Keen, John Fleming, Teddie Smith, C. L. Fitzjames, T. E. Bolton, J. Metcalfe and C. Colburn.

Silverdale Home Guard 1945. Back row L–R: Frank Bolton, Thomas Holmes, Amos Hodgson, unknown, unknown, Archie Fletcher, Tommy Holmes, Len Clark, Jack Lambert, Walter Dobson, Ray Holmes, Syd Walker, John Walker. Mid row: unknown, unknown, Yorkie Richmond, Richard Knowles, Miles Mason, Syd Newton, Reg Kaye. Front row: Gerald Richardson, John W. Walker, Bill Simpson, Joe Hawkins.

Home Guard Rifle Team: Cup Winners 1943–44. Back row L–R: John Walker, Walter Dobson. Mid row: Miles Mason, Richard Knowles (CO), Archie Fletcher. Front rwow: John W. Walker, Bill Simpson and Joe Hawkins.

The Home Guard Pipe and Drum Band practising on the shore in 1944.

Victory Parade outside the Gaskell Hall in 1945. In the overcoat is Sir Ian Frazer (local MP and founder of the RNIB) with Major Wilkinson. Miss Hinchcliffe is talking to Sir Ian. Behind them are Jack Holmes (wearing a helmet) Betty Walker, Mrs Booth, Edith Winterbottom. Mr Lacy, the postmaster, is standing in a trilby to the left.

The Silverdale village War Memorial carved by Frank Bolton. In 1921 it listed 27 Silverdalians who paid the ultimate price in the Great War.

The village memorial was unveiled by Colonel Wadham of Dalton in 1921. The site was donated by Mr F. J. Dickens of the Woodlands and the memorial itself was hand carved in Stainton Limestone by Frank Bolton. The ceremony was preceded by a short service conducted by the vicar in the Parish Church. The large congregation proceeded in procession to the memorial site. Colonel Wadham unveiled the cross, which had been covered in a large Union Jack. The Last Post was sounded by buglers from the King's Own Regiment. Colonel Wadham afterwards distributed bronze medals to relatives of the fallen and the ex-servicemen. The National Anthem concluded the ceremony.

Both faces of the bronze medal provided by the Peace Council Committee and distributed by Colonel Wadham. The originals are just over one inch in diameter and very few appear to have survived to the present day.

The original cross blew down in a gale in 1960. In 1962 it was pieced together and laid in front of the plinth. A new plain Latin Cross was added in June 1979, the funds being raised by public subscription. The photograph shows the erection of the new cross, with Cecil Lockwood, the Chairman of Parish Council, Mrs Lockwood, and Frank Bolton the stonemason (right).

Those remembered on the
Silverdale and Lindeth war memorial

First World War

Name, age   **Regiment/service location**

Allinson, John, 21
16th October, 1918
1st Battalion, North Staffordshire Regiment
Killed in action near Cambrai

Ambrose, Henry, 29
18th July, 1916
8th Battalion, King's Own Royal Lancaster Regiment
Killed in action at Longueval during the Battle of the Somme

Bell, George Arthur, 21
31st July, 1917
18th Battalion, Manchester Regiment
Killed in action during the Third Battle of Ypres

Benjamin, William, 34
24th/30th September, 1916
31st Battalion, Canadian Infantry (Alberta Regiment)
Killed in action at Courcelette during the Battle of the Somme

Bolton, William Henry, 33
17th April, 1918
2nd Battalion, Auckland Regiment, New Zealand Forces
Killed in action near Hebuterne on the Somme battlefield

Bolton, James Richard, 18
10th October, 1918
53rd (Graduated) Battalion, King's Liverpool Regiment
Died of pneumonia in camp at Conway in North Wales

Braithwaite, John, 24
11th October, 1917
7th Battalion, Seaforth Highlanders
Died of wounds at a Casualty Clearing Station in the Third Battle of Ypres

Champion, Eric Osborne, 21
11th June 1917
11th Battalion, South Lancashire Regiment
Killed by shellfire while in billets near Zillebeke in the Ypres Salient

Clark, Thomas Postlethwaite, 35
3rd September, 1916
2nd Battalion, King's Own Scottish Borderers
Killed in action at Delville Wood during the Battle of the Somme

Cornthwaite, John, 27
7th July, 1918

'B' Battery, 92nd Brigade, Royal Field Artillery
Died of wounds at a Casualty Clearing Station near Arras

Dobson, Ingram, 25
12th December, 1915

31st Battalion, Canadian Infantry (Alberta Regiment)
Died of wounds at a Casualty Clearing Station near Ypres

Edmondson, Frederick, 20
6th June, 1916

12th Battalion, Rifle Brigade (Prince Consort's Own)
Killed in action at Potijze in the Ypres Salient

Farrar, Lucien, 21
13th January, 1918

1st/4th Battalion, Loyal North Lancashire Regiment
Died as a prisoner of war in Germany of wounds received near Épehy.

Graham, Thomas Abba, 29
9th February, 1917

6th Battalion, King's Own Royal Lancaster Regiment
Killed in action at Kut al Amara, Mesopotamia (Iraq)

Hebden, Reginald Ronald Hope, 28
9th April, 1917

78th Battalion, Canadian Infantry (Manitoba Regiment)
Killed in action at Vimy Ridge during the Battle of Arras

Hayton, John, 33
24th October, 1916

50th Battalion, Canadian Infantry (Alberta Regiment)
Died of wounds at a Base Hospital at Etaples, France

Hayton, John William, 21
26th February, 1917

1st Battalion, Royal Welsh Fusiliers
Killed in action by shellfire near Serre on the Somme battlefield

Horn, Jonathan, 31
14th January, 1918

2nd Battalion, Rifle Brigade (Prince Consort's Own)
Killed in action near Wieltje in the Ypres Salient

Holden, Thomas Henry, 24
4th August, 1917

8th Battalion, Loyal North Lancashire Regiment
Killed in action on the Westhoek Ridge during the Third Battle of Ypres

Keen, George William, 25
16th August, 1915

1st/5th Battalion, King's Own Royal Lancaster Regiment
Killed in action near Wytschaete in the Ypres Salient

Lambert, Gilbert Harley, 25
16th June 1917

15th Battalion, Australian Infantry
Died of wounds at a Casualty Clearing Station near Ypres

Martindale, William, 19
1st July, 1916

2nd Battalion, Border Regiment
Died of wounds at a Casualty Station during the Battle of the Somme

Moss, Richard, 32
13th September, 1917

1st/4th Battalion, King's Own Royal Lancaster Regiment
Died of sickness at the Base Hospital at St Omer

Richmond, Charles Leo, 24
19th November, 1916

2nd Battalion, Irish Guards
Killed in action by shellfire near Ginchy on the Somme battlefield

Smith, Cecil Ramsden, 27
12th June, 1917

'M' Special Company, Royal Engineers
Killed in action near Armentières

Walker, William Halkett, 27
26th October, 1917

2nd/5th Battalion, King's Own Royal Lancaster Regiment
Killed in action at Poelcapelle during the Third Battle of Ypres

*Not shown on the village War Memorial but listed on the St John's Church memorial dedicated on the 24th March 1924

***Edmondson** Tyson
28th March 1918

1st Battalion New Zealand Expeditionary Force
Killed on the Somme

Second World War

Name, age	**Regiment/service location**

Briggs, John Maurice Winnington, 25
10th May, 1945

1409 (Meteorological) Flight, Royal Air Force
Died in an air crash in Canada while on a post-VE Day victory tour

Hall, Cecil William, 31
28th May, 1944

2nd Battalion, Coldstream Guards
Killed in action at the Battle of Monte Cassino in Italy

Hewitson, Kenneth, 21
22nd September, 1943

218 Squadron, Royal Air Force Volunteer Reserve
Shot down over Neustadt-am-Rübenberge while on a raid on Germany

9

LOOKING AFTER THE VISITORS

THE ARRIVAL OF THE RAILWAY IN 1857 dramatically increased the number of visitors to the village. For the first time Silverdale became accessible to those on more modest incomes living in the industrial districts of the north. The people of Bradford, particularly, were attracted to sea bathing, pleasure boating and the beautiful scenery of the northern part of Morecambe Bay. The people of Silverdale were quick to recognise the potential for additional income by providing accommodation, catering, shops and recreation for the summer visitors.

For the best part of 100 years, facilities in the village grew to meet the needs of the visitors and the increasing local population. Many of the private houses in the village offered some form of accommodation, boasting such luxuries as indoor sanitation, electricity, mains water and pianos. There were up to four hotels: the Silverdale, the Royal, Mountain View and the Woodlands. At the peak there were fourteen shops including a bank and a 'circulating library'. In addition there were between eight and ten travelling traders visiting the village each week. Ten of the local farmers were delivering fresh milk.

Bolton's Cafe & Car Park. Silverdale.

There were numerous cafés located all round the village. Bolton's Café on Shore Road was one of the largest and was closest to the beach. When it closed in 1946 a second storey was added and it is now a dwelling house close to the shore cattle-grid.

Opposite top: across from the Silverdale Hotel was Moorby's Ices Cabin. Bill Moorby, seen here, lived on Lindeth Road where his wife ran North Lindeth boarding house.

Opposite: Young Joe Walker outside Agnes Walker's Tea Room in the lean-to at Croft Cottage on Stankeld Road. In recent years the cottage has been much altered and is now known as Pointer House.

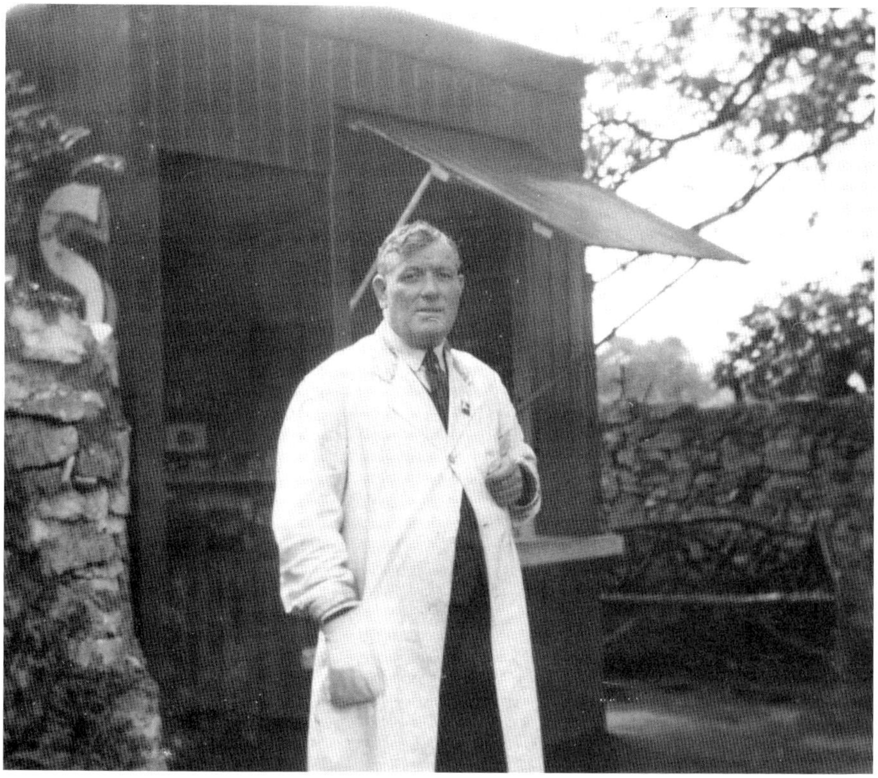

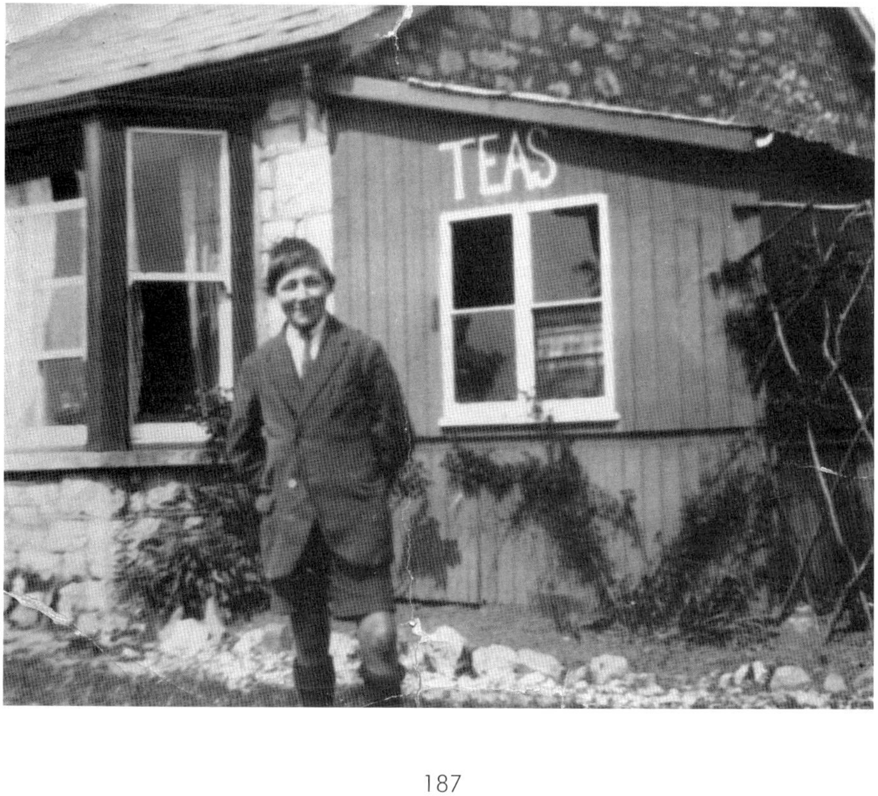
TEAS

The Silverdale Hotel (formerly the Britannia) with customers arriving by the coach load. Note the wooden billiard room next to the main building.

Changing times at the Silverdale Hotel as the motorcar began to replace horse-drawn vehicles. Here we see old and new, horse and chauffeur-driven car, with Henry Thornton of Yew Tree House in the rear, with Doris Thwaite, daughter of the landlady, Mrs Emily Thwaite (née Hall) standing by the left pillar. Meanwhile Dearman James is holding a horse called Snowden (July 1910).

The hotel was built in 1826 and was known as the Britannia. Coaches were garaged in through the arch of the adjacent coach house and there was a five-bay stable to the rear. This building was subsequently converted into a squash court before becoming a dwelling house. The walnut tree overhanging Shore Road on the right was felled as late as 1990.

Tom Bolton and Sam Letcher enjoying a quiet pint in the hotel bar.

View from Silverdale Hotel Across Morecambe Bay

The original view as seen from the hotel. Much of the land in front of the hotel was later developed as Shore Close and most of the view across the bay was lost.

Until Shore Close was developed there was an outdoor swimming pool in the grounds of the Silverdale Hotel.

Now an annex to a boys' school, Cumbria View started out as a private residence called Oak Lea. In the 1920s it was converted into a hotel known as Mountain View. In 1958 an extension was built to the main house for a Masonic Lodge.

Adverts for the Mountain View Hotel showing the interior in the 1930s, taken from the local brochure 'Silverdale: The Loveliest Spot on Morecambe Bay', published by the Silverdale Advancement Association, made up of local business people, and the brochure was printed by Thomas Richmond, the local newsagent. It was sold for two old pence.

Tea Room and Cocktail Bar.

Mountain View Hotel

THIS HOTEL is in the heart of England's most glorious country overlooking the Lake District mountains. The Hotel Gardens, Putting Green and Tennis Court are beautifully laid out and are seen from the Drawing Room and all main Bedrooms.

Guests may rely on Excellent Service and Cuisine

TERMS PER DAY INCLUDES :
Table d'Hote Breakfast
Hot Lunch or Cold Sideboard
Afternoon Tea
Dinner
Room and Attendance

Sandwiches are provided if required when out for Lunch

TELEPHONES
MANAGEMENT : 254   VISITORS : 271

Mountain View
Licensed Residential
Hotel
SILVERDALE
via Carnforth

A Modern Hotel   Excellent Cooking
 Most convenient for Lake District
H. & C. all Rooms   Electric Light

Good Garage Accommodation

PROPRIETORS : MR. & MRS. SCHOFIELD

In 1945 the Woodlands became a hotel providing accommodation for visitors. Later it became a private residence again but the bar continued to operate. Today it is an award-winning hostelry much loved by locals and visitors alike.

The Woodlands drawing room in 1942, just before the house became a hotel.

Bay View House on Stankelt Road offering 'Board Residence and Apartments with indoor sanitation'. The rather stern-looking lady at the front gate is Mrs Pennell, the proprietress. In the village in the 1930s there were some thirty houses offering accommodation, apartments or rentals. Less formal B&B was also available at many homes in the village.

Accommodation was to be found at virtually all the Shore Cottages. The larger house at the end of the row was known as Bath Cottage where Miss Hinchliffe offered board residence with 'home comforts'. The number of deck chairs shows that the Shore Cottages were very popular.

Dowthwaite's Refreshment Rooms opposite the library (after 1911). Mr Dowthwaite, leaning on window sill, arranged for visitors to be picked up from the trains at the station or from steamers on the shore. They went on a scenic tour that just happened to end up at his refreshment rooms before returning home.

The menu for Dowthwaite's Refreshment Rooms, a menu very much of its time with no vegetables or salads in sight.

Mrs. DOWTHWAITE'S Refreshment Rooms, CHURCH ROAD, SILVERDALE.

ALL OF THE BEST QUALITY.
TARIFF.

	s.	d.
Cup of freshly made Tea		1½
Pot of freshly made Tea (2 cups)		4
Tea with bread & butter and preserves		6
Tea with sweets		8
Tea with egg and bread & butter		8
Tea with ham and bread & butter		10
Tea with ham and egg and bread & butter	1	0
Tea with steak and bread and butter	1	0
Tea with chop and bread and butter	1	0
Plate of bread & butter		3
Buttered Scone		1½
Sandwich		2

Special Hot Dinners to order.
Picnic Parties catered for on the shortest notice.
GOOD ACCOMMODATION FOR CYCLISTS.
GOOD STABLING

CIGARS
CIGARETTES
TOBACCOS

Passengers alighting in the courtyard behind Dowthwaite's with the serving staff waiting to greet the customers. This must have been taken about 1903 before Bleasdale House was extended up to the roadside, and before the coach house, stables and billiard room across the road were built.

Allinson's Refreshment Rooms at Grove House on Shore Road. The sign over the door says that it was licensed! The photo, taken by Frank Crosland of Arnside, probably dates from about 1900. The present Walker's Garage and the Silverdale Hotel can be seen further up Shore Road.

Wayside Tea Gardens at Church Cottage on Emesgate. The proprietor, Alberta Johnson and her mother are seen seated. In later years it was a sweet shop and there are those in the village today who still remember buying sweets before crossing the road to school.

Cunliffe's Café on Holborn (now the Newsagent and Post Office). The photo was taken in 1903 long before the Gaskell Hall was completed in 1931. The open field can be seen just beyond Mr Knight's butcher shop.

Steamers brought day-trippers from Morecambe and Grange on the tide. The local fishermen made a few pence ferrying the visitors ashore. The steamer seen here was the Morecambe Queen, a mussel boat, modified to carry passengers during the summer but still used for musseling in the winter (1907).

Prawners and small fishing boats offered pleasure trips around the bay when the tide permitted. Edith Hindle can be seen here in the foreground watching two boats setting off in 1905.

Children swimming close to the shore in 1903. This was a card sent to young George Keen when he was a child asking 'could he see himself' in the photograph. Son of the local painting contractor, Townson Keen, George was subsequently killed in WWI and his name is on the village war memorial.

Bathers in one of the channels on the sands between The Cove and Shore Road (1939). As dangerous an activity then as it is today.

Camping between Know Hill Farm and Bolton's Café in the 1930s.

Donkey rides on Silverdale shore! Mr Robinson, who had the livery stables and blacksmith shop behind Old Forge Cottage on Emesgate Lane, kept donkeys and it is probably him leading the children along the shore.

Picnicking on the shore in about 1910.

Well-dressed visitors in their 'Sunday Best,' and although they visited for many years, in this instance they do not look too pleased to be here. They lodged in Springbank and this card dates from the 1950s.

Crossing the sands with a local guide and two options, dry feet or wet! (1950s)

The Retreat, next to Silverdale Tennis Club, in 1936. The Retreat was a convalescent home for the poor and sick of the Bradford Parish, Manchester, and was run by the Misses Harrison and Martin. The building, located close to what is now the entrance to Hazelwood, was used until about 1960 when the farmer sold the land for building. The tennis courts were located on the flat ground between Hazelwood and Clarence House.

ACKNOWLEDGEMENTS

The fact that this volume is dedicated to the late John Bolton is a clear recognition of his extensive research on the history of Silverdale. He was generous in his support and allowed me ready access to his large collection of photos and notes.

A book such as this could not have been produced without the help and co-operation of many people. I would like to express my gratitude to those many individuals who have willingly shared their memories of Silverdale and/or have lent me photographs and postcards.

Particular thanks go to Margaret Pearson and her late mother 'Aunty Bel'. My appreciation goes to the following: Ruth Redman, Margaret Brown, Angela Chatburn, Jim Bolton, the late Hilda Letcher, and John Walker – what a mine of information! Thanks are also due to the following villagers who loaned personal material and were happy talk about old Silverdale: Brenda Farrar, Walter Burrow, Jill Mason, Jane Lambert, Wal and Jill Park, Linda Kaye, Marie Rafferty, Brian Dobson, Carole Lithgow, Carol Devlin, Rodney Doldon, Audrey Mason, Margaret Fryer, Dawn Sharples, Tim Proctor, Hazel Quirk, Jenny Ashworth, Jenny Agar, Bobby Barber, Marie Motch, Ann Turnbull, Wyn Glover, the late Teresa Richmond, Jack and Pat Simpson.

I am indebted to Mike Moon for access to his extensive collection of Silverdale postcards and the late Barry Ayre, former editor of *Keer to Kent* magazine, for permission to use his large archive of local material. Special thanks are due to Angela Redman and Grenville Fletcher for making available Leeds Children's Holiday Centre archives.

I am grateful to Jill Mason of Silverdale Library, John Rogan of Morecambe Local Studies Library and the staff of Lancaster City Library who have provided much background information. Thanks to the archivists at Lancashire County Records Office for facilitating access to the Enid Parkin collection and other Silverdale records.

Personal thanks are due to Margaret Pearson for reviewing the manuscript and Wal Park for proof reading.

Finally I acknowledge the unending support of my wife, Ann, throughout the years I have been working on this book.